Welcome to Hawkes!

Practical skills in reading and writing are necessary for students of all disciplines both during and beyond their college years. The *Reading and Writing Handbook* provides straightforward, relevant, and easy-to-find answers to students' questions about reading, writing, grammar, mechanics, and research.

As one of the first to utilize our pilot release of the *Reading and Writing Handbook*, you play a valuable role in the continued development of this text. We encourage and appreciate your input. Please email **English@hawkeslearning.com** to let us know what you think and to learn about further opportunities for reviewing our English offerings.

Sincerely,

KCleveland

Katherine Cleveland
English Project Coordinator

Reading & Writing
HANDBOOK
for the College Student

Pilot Edition
* Content Subject To Change *

Executive Editor: Katherine Cleveland
Editors: Laura Brown, Caitlin Edahl

Lead Designer: Tee Jay Zajac
Designers: Bryan Mitchell, James Smalls, Patrick Thompson

VP Research & Development: Marcel Prevuznak
VP of Marketing: Emily Cook

A division of Quant Systems, Inc.

546 Long Point Road, Mount Pleasant, SC 29464

Printed in the United States of America

ISBN: 978-1-944894-72-6

Table of Contents

Part 1   Reading and Writing

Part 2   Effective Sentences

Part 4   Punctuation and Mechanics

Part 5   Research

1

PART 1

Reading and Writing

Chapter 1

Thinking Critically

Reading critically does not mean that you're looking for flaws or that you're trying to find errors in someone's work. Instead, to be *critical* means to decode or make sense of a text to find its meaning and relevance.

Reading critically goes beyond the words and determines how and why the text is put together and who the intended audience is.

Critical reading and critical writing are connected. Learning and practicing strategies for reading critically will help you to write critically. As you learn to recognize the parts of a text, you will have a better grasp on how to write a text that impacts your readers.

1a Critical Reading Process

Reading critically has five major steps:

1. Previewing
2. Reading
3. Marking and annotating
4. Analyzing
5. Evaluating

Previewing

Before you start reading, skim over the text. Read the title and any subheadings, examine paragraph arrangement and transitions, identify the thesis, and look for bold words. Then, create a list of questions for the text.

Write down your questions and expectations for that section. Here are some example questions:

- What can I learn from the main title and section titles?
- How is the text organized?

- What is the author's argument?
- Where is the most important evidence located?
- What is the organizational pattern?
- Is the thesis clear? Do I agree with it?
- What action does the author expect the audience to take?
- Is there any obvious bias?

Reading

Plan a time to read through the text without interruptions. In order to focus effectively, read at a reliable time and place. Afterward, review your outline and see which questions you can answer. Also write down first impressions, including your response to the text as a whole.

When you are drafting these notes, don't worry about formal writing conventions. Write in a way that makes sense to you and that you can understand at a later point. Here are some examples of responses:

> Author is opposed to the new gun control laws, wants it repealed—no attempt to control bias
>
> Wait time is too restrictive
>
> Emphasizes mental health care reform
>
> Cites lawsuit
>
> Cites NRA president
>
> Thesis statement is strong but only two main points seem fully developed
>
> Suggests new standards for background checks
>
> Criticizes senator's comment
>
> Cites second amendment

After you're done with these notes, re-read them as a way to summarize the reading and your critique of it.

Marking and Annotating the Text

Marking a text will help you find important information more quickly. Use marks or symbols that you can remember, such as stars, dots, question marks, or checkmarks.

Annotating simply means adding notes to something. Remember, highlighting by itself doesn't usually work. If you simply highlight a sentence while reading, you may not remember why it's highlighted when you come back to it later. Instead, write words in the margins. Here are some examples of annotations:

> Important point
>
> Thesis
>
> What does this mean?
>
> Seems to disagree
>
> Solid support!
>
> Check facts
>
> Author seems biased here
>
> Personal experience supports thesis

Using symbols and annotations will make your notes meaningful and easy to understand.

Take a look at this text, marked and annotated by a student:

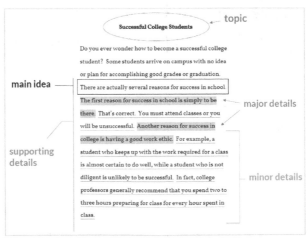

Figure 1.1

Analyzing Content

To **analyze** means to examine carefully. This is a major part of critical reading. To analyze a text, re-read it slowly and closely to see how the text and its argument are developed and supported. Look for ideas that are repeated or an overarching theme.

Every text is writing for an intended **purpose**, or goal, and for a specific **audience**. Asking questions about these elements will help you analyze the text.

Here are some questions to ask yourself about a text's purpose:

- What is the format of the text? Why might the author have chosen it?
- What does the argument appear to be?
- What action does the author want the reader to take?
- How does the author seem to feel about the opposition?
- How are my previous ideas challenged by the author's argument?
- What evidence is offered, and what does the author suggest this evidence proves?

If you can identify the purpose, it will help you make sense of the text's meaning and the deliberate choices that the author made.

Here are some questions to ask yourself about a text's audience:

- Who is the author addressing?
- How does the word choice seem to speak to a specific group of people?
- What does the author think I already know?
- If a problem is presented, does the author imply that someone is responsible for it?
- What caused the situation being discussed?

Remember that if you're reading a text, you're part of the current audience. However, authors often write to an intended audience as well. For example, when C.S. Lewis wrote the essays in *Mere Christianity*, his intended audience may have been people living in Britain in the 1940s. However, today his current audience is made up of people all over the world.

Evaluating the Evidence

If the text you're reading is making an argument, it will be filled with evidence supporting that argument. Read and re-read the text closely to determine whether the evidence is credible, logical, and consistent.

Here are some questions to ask yourself about a text's evidence:

- Is there enough evidence to support this claim thoroughly?
- Is the evidence biased?
- What sources is the author using for support? Are they reliable?
- What can I find out about the facts and statistics in the text?
- Is there any background information available for the author?

Let's take a look at an example of a student's annotations on an article about gun control. This student has completed all five steps of the critical reading process.

Debunking means changing common ideas, so the purpose of the text is probably to persuade.

Debunking Misperceptions about Gun Control

Media coverage of violence is often spun as a red flag indicating the need for more restrictive gun laws. While this is probably comforting for gun opponents, it's clearly media manipulation to push their own agenda. News reporters and pundits focus on the weapon when the person operating it is responsible. Tighter gun control laws actually create more hazardous communities by encouraging a criminal mindset, preventing self-defense, and building an environment of fear.

Criminal Intent

Obviously, many gun-related incidents involve criminals who aren't deterred by laws. More laws and restrictions are not going to hinder someone who isn't concerned about illegal behavior. Laws control those who agree to abide by them. Even those perpetrators without a criminal history make the conscious choice to break a law. Rewriting legislation or stiffening penalties is unlikely to change their minds.

Without a gun, determined criminals will find other ways to carry out their plan, whether with a knife or other "unregulated" weapons. If they're prepared to take lives, a home-made bomb is an obvious choice to kill hundreds of people. We've seen far too many examples of this. Tools are always available to those who want them.

Punish the Victim

Gun control punishes innocent, law-abiding people by restricting their access to self-defense and the right to protect their families. This is a violation of our liberties as Americans. If it's illegal to own a gun as a private citizen, we have to depend on police for their protection. The last time I called police in response to a break-in, it took over thirty minutes for them to arrive. I was vulnerable and unsure whether the burglar was still in the area, watching me.

Disarming citizens is exactly what criminals want, and the media is playing right into their hands. It helps the predator to disarm the prey. Under these circumstances, criminals could run rampant because most people would have no access to self-defense.

Results in Reverse

Furthermore, cities with the strictest gun control laws have the highest incident rates for violent crimes. Those laws make it safe for criminals by turning citizens into prey. Areas with more legally armed citizens tend to decrease crime. For instance, when Kennesaw, Georgia, passed an ordinance requiring every adult to have one gun in the home, burglaries ultimately decreased by 89%. Clearly, criminals don't want to break into a residence and risk being killed.

Looking at the title and subsections makes me think that the author wants looser gun laws.

Based on a first reading, the author is opposed to banning private access to guns. The author also seems to think that people who believe in gun restriction have been manipulated by the media. I'd assume that the author is a gun advocate.

Analyzing the text shows that the author has had a bad experience with police response time to a crime

I think the audience is probably voters who are undecided about gun control. The author assumes his audience is familiar with the Oregon shooting. Written recently?

> The author might be supporting gun training in this third section. He also quotes a CNN interview. Is this source credible? Look this up!

> In a recent CNN interview, gun advocate John Lott has pointed out that most "mass shootings occur in areas where guns are banned, where citizens are unable to go and defend themselves" (Lott CNN).

> There's no clear conclusion, but the author seems to be trying to convince readers that access to guns is a good thing.

1b Determining the Purpose of a Text

Thinking about a text's purpose answers the *why* question: "Why was this text written?"

Possible answers may link one or more of these actions with a particular topic:

To respond	To propose
To describe	To compare/contrast
To inform	To summarize
To argue/persuade	To evaluate
To discuss	To entertain
To analyze	To recommend

Many texts are not *only* informative; they usually try to make a claim about an issue or idea. Even personal narratives often express a certain perspective or convey a life lesson.

Determining the purpose of a text begins with analyzing its key components and asking *how* and *why* questions about these components. Some purposes can be determined through simple questions, while others need more complex investigation.

Here are some hints to help you to determine the purpose of a text:

Title and Subheadings

Titles and subheadings in some writing formats state the purpose right away. Here are some examples:

Five Reasons Why You Should Vote Libertarian

Recommendations for Budget Cuts

Marketing Strategy for 2017

Thesis Statements or Purpose Statements

A **thesis** or **purpose statement** should appear in the introduction or first paragraph. These statements express the main idea of the longer work, which is often a claim or perspective that the author is defending.

Call to Action

Find the call to action, usually in the conclusion and/or introduction. Sometimes, authors will repeat this for emphasis throughout a piece of writing.

Here are some questions to ask yourself about the call to action:

- What action is the author advising the reader to take?
- Does the author want the audience to accept his or her perspective?

Organization

Organization patterns often provide clues about purpose. Cause and effect or order of importance organization is often used to argue, evaluate, or analyze. Spatial organization is used to describe. If items are being compared and contrasted, the purpose may be to recommend or evaluate. Chronological order probably indicates that the purpose is to summarize.

Here are some questions to ask about the organization:

- What organizational pattern can I identify?
- Why is this text arranged in this order?
- Where is the most important evidence likely to be located?
- How does the use of this pattern support the author's purpose for writing?

Transitions

Conclusion transitions often guide the reader back to the thesis, which may be re-stated or paraphrased. Words like *clearly* and *obviously* or a phrase like "the evidence indicates" point to the author's argument.

Let's take a look at an example of a student's annotations while reading an article on organic eating. This student's annotations focus on identifying and analyzing purpose

This title is pretty neutral; no clues about purpose or audience.

Organic Options

While the organic movement may seem a recent (and even sudden) national obsession, the idea began gaining ground since the 1960s, and revived with the retro movement of the 1990s. Celebrities have promoted "natural" products, and farmers' markets have become popular for buying and selling home-grown foods and textiles. Organic products are more popular than ever, but this is beyond a hipster trend. When we examine the benefits at both the micro and macro levels, organic alternatives are the right choice for individuals and for the earth.

The thesis seems to make an argument for "organic alternatives"

One reason so many people have opted for the organic lifestyle is to eliminate allergy-triggering chemical compounds from their diets. Imagine cutting 70% of the chemicals and pesticides found in conventional foods. This is a significant change that seems to improve energy, stabilize digestive function, and reduce headaches in many individuals. Removing chemical additives from our diet improves brain function and mood, and since organic food is not genetically modified (GMO), the levels of nutrients and vitamins in these foods is higher and healthier.

However, vegetarians aren't the only ones who benefit. Organic meat comes from livestock raised without hormones, antibiotics, or other growth-enhancing products. Keeping these substances out of the animals' food makes the dairy, eggs, and meat products healthier for human consumption as well. If we're feeding growth hormones to animals to make them larger, it should be no surprise that our country has an obesity problem.

It's hard to imagine why any human would choose to consume preservatives when we see the effect of preservatives on food. In one study, a meal of French fries and a burger took three weeks to grow mold, demonstrating that this type of food is so full of preservatives that it doesn't decompose naturally. Chemical preservatives in food negatively impact our bodies and our offspring, but perhaps more irreversible damage is done to our water sources and soil.

Evidence from a study showing the effect of preservatives; builds the argument more

Healthy eating is only the tip of the iceberg. We make that choice. But regardless of what we prefer to eat, biodegradability and the quest for sustainable resources are environmental issues that affect us all. Unlike humans, the earth doesn't get to choose what it absorbs. The renewability of natural resources is impacted by chemical pesticides and inorganic compounds.

The first sentence of this new paragraph gives a clue about order of importance. This appears to be the author's subtle argument: persuading us to buy organic foods because of the long-term effects on society and the world.

Context

Context may offer clues about purpose. Some texts that *appear* to be written only for information or entertainment—like narratives, research papers, editorials, and blog posts—require a bit more investigation to find the purpose. Often, focusing on the context of the text can help.

Here are some questions to ask yourself about a text's context:

- When and where was the text written?
- Who is the author and what do I know about his/her views?
- Where was the author born and under what circumstances?
- What key events or circumstances (culture, religion, war, politics, family, loss) might have prompted the writing?

Author background information offers a valuable filter for answering questions about purpose. Time, place, family, loss, culture, experience, and circumstances can all provide answers for why an author writes.

For example, why did Mary Shelley write *Frankenstein*, a story about an abandoned, childlike, and unnatural creature? This background information offers a number of answers.

On a stormy summer night in 1816, after telling ghost stories with friends, Mary Shelley began writing *Frankenstein*. The previous summer, she had given birth prematurely to a daughter who only lived for two weeks. Mary had tried to revive the baby by massaging its chest in front of a fire. When Mary herself was two weeks old, her own mother died. She often wrote of feeling "abandoned" by her father, philosopher William Godwin. One of Godwin's close friends, Erasmus Darwin (Charles Darwin's grandfather), lectured and wrote about the source of life and possibility of evolution. Shelley's husband had published *Prometheus Unbound*, a play about the Greek mythological bearer of fire.

Tone

Tone may offer clues about purpose. **Tone** is the author's positive, negative, or neutral attitude toward the topic.

Here are some questions to ask yourself about a text's tone:

- How does the author appear to feel toward the topic (positive, negative, neutral)?
- What specific words could describe this tone?
- Does the author emphasize certain words and phrases?
- What adverbs, adjectives, and figures of speech are used?
- If a problem or conflict has been described in the text, how does the author seem to feel toward the situation? Does s/he offer a solution?

1c Determining the Audience of a Text

Despite who is reading a text, the author probably had a specific audience in mind while writing. This is no different than when you write a paper, text message, or email to a specific audience.

Determining who an author is writing for will help you understand the purpose of the text and the context. Several components of the text offer hints about the intended audience.

Language, Style, and Word Choice

Language, style, and word choice suggest an author's intended audience. In conversation and in writing, you naturally adapt your vocabulary and conversational style according to the people you want to reach. For example, technical terms and longer, more complex sentences could indicate that the intended audience is made up of experts in that topic.

Here are some questions to ask yourself about a text's language, style, and word choice:

- Is the language relatable and easy to understand, or highly technical?

- Is the word choice welcoming, aggressive, or in-between?

- How often did I need to look up words?

- Are there words or phrases that are repeated often?

- Are there words or phrases that can connect to a particular idea?

- What relationship does the author appear to have with the audience?

- Does the author use inclusive pronouns like *we* and *us*? If so, where and how?

Consider the ways your word choice and style might change when you're communicating with these people:

- A close friend
- An elderly neighbor
- A coworker
- Your manager
- Your parents
- An instructor
- A date
- A group of trainees
- Your doctor

Content

Content choices hint at the intended audience by either assuming prior knowledge or providing necessary background information on the topic. Complicated background details or assumptions indicate a more sophisticated or informed audience.

Here are some questions to ask yourself about a text's content:

- What information does the author include?
- In what way(s) is this information supported?
- Are the sources of supporting evidence reliable and understandable?
- What appears to be missing?
- Are opposing views acknowledged?
- Was I familiar with at least some of the information before I read it?
- Did the author attempt to establish some common knowledge before beginning the argument?

Exercise

The following are two excerpts from texts intended for different audiences. Given the content and language used in each text, what can you determine about the intended audience for each article? Write your response in the space below.

Sample 1

Intelligence: New Findings and Theoretical Developments

Studies estimate the heritability of IQ is somewhere between .4 and .8, but it really makes no sense to talk about a single value for the heritability of intelligence. The heritability of a trait depends on the relative variances of the predictors, in this case genotype and environment. The concept of herItability has its origins in animal breeding . . . In free-ranging humans, however, variability is uncontrolled, there is no "true" degree of variation to estimate, and heritability can take practically any value for any trait . . .

(excerpt from an article written by a group of psychologists and published in 2012 in *American Psychologist*)

Language: Fact based. Requires some prior knowledge. Several terms I might have to look up. Some complex sentences.

Content: Background information assumed. Cites .4 vs. .8 variables – not sure what scale.

Intended Audience:

Sample 2

The Relationship Between Genetics and Intelligence

Some people have an IQ similar to that of their parents. In this case, we might ask ourselves whether genetics and environment both play a role in impacting IQ scores. The simple answer is this: yes. Research are working to discern the impact of household, heredity, or both. Some studies performed by psychologists show that genetics account for only half of an individual's intelligence. Therefore, many of them believe that the environment in which a person is raised has a strong influence on IQ scores.

Language: Adult but more readable. Nothing to look up. Refers to psychologists and geneticists as "them." Refers to "we" and "our" kids with simple sentences.

Content: Background information provided. Uses general, simple information.

Intended Audience:

Chapter 2

The Writing Process

The Writing Process is more than just a list of steps to follow when you set out to complete a writing assignment. It is a formula that will help you develop clear ideas, informed arguments, and an overall more unified and polished piece of writing.

You can adapt the writing process to fit your needs as a writer, but following all of the steps can really help you think through what you want to say, how you want to say it, and the best way to present that information to your audience.

Writing is more than just correct grammar and proper sentence structure; writing allows you to express your ideas and feelings about any topic. Following the steps of this process will help you to do both.

The Six Steps of the Writing Process

1. Pre-writing
2. Reading and Research
3. Drafting
4. Revising
5. Editing
6. Reflecting

2a Pre-Writing

Pre-writing is the first step of the writing process. This is the time to brainstorm, come up with ideas, and decide which topics you can really get excited about. Writing about something that isn't important to you is tedious for you *and* for your audience, who can probably tell that you are not very interested in your topic.

Luckily, there are several ways to pre-write. You may need to return to this step several times during your process, as it can be also used to develop small or supporting ideas.

Different Methods of Pre-Writing:

- Listing
- Mind-mapping
- Free-writing
- Questioning

Listing

One of the most helpful ways to begin thinking about your paper is to make lists. You can list questions you have, sources you want to use, or key words that you are thinking about exploring in your research. Either way, lists help you get your thoughts on paper and get organized to move forward.

Mind-Mapping

Another pre-writing method is mind-mapping: making a web to show different ideas that all relate to your main topic. Your lists may evolve into a chart like this one below:

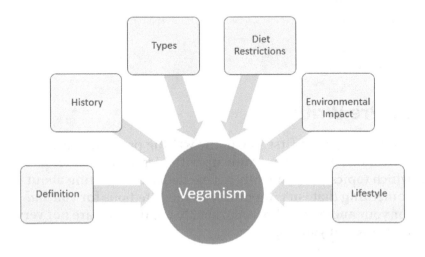

Figure 1.2

Exercise

Now try this strategy for yourself. If you have a current assignment in the pre-writing phase, write your potential topic in the middle of the space below. If you are in-between writings, choose a topic of interest to you. Then, fill in the boxes with related ideas. Feel free to add more boxes if you have more ideas! There is no limit with brainstorming.

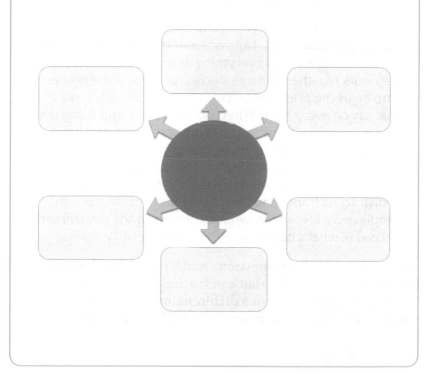

Free-Writing

Sometimes, the best pre-writing method is to free-write and see what comes out. This means writing or typing for a planned amount of time (maybe five to ten minutes) and letting the ideas and questions flow.

After your time is up, read what you wrote and circle the ideas that have potential. Then, complete a more focused free-write, focusing on the ideas you circled.

Take a look at the following writing prompt and the resulting passage from a student who completed free-writing about the provided subject.

Assignment: Write a research paper on a current event or popular trend that you find perplexing. Draw from trending topics you see on social media and on television, but make sure it is something you can research well (search the library website to ensure there are applicable sources). Start with a ten minute free-writing session.

Free-Write: I've always wanted to know more about how the government works. I know about the different branches and the president and everything, but I want to know how they work together to make decisions. What is the process? Who helps the president decide? Does he actually have the final say on everything? When do the Senate and Congress step in? I want to know how the process works and how things actually get done or get prevented from being done in this country. Why isn't there more news on this process instead of celebrity gossip? Is the gossip supposed to distract us from something? Why aren't the American people more involved in what's going on in the government instead of what's happening on their favorite TV shows?

As you can see, asking questions and letting ideas flow often leads to other questions that can further develop your topic. You may even end up with a different topic, but as long as you're still following assignment guidelines, that's fine.

Questioning

As you think about your paper, you will naturally have questions about your topic.

Take a look at a student's questions about the topic of refugees in Europe and the Middle East. Notice that the list does not need to be formal as long as *you* understand it.

Where are different refugees coming from?

Why are they leaving their homes?

How do they find safety?

What happens to their family members that are left behind?

Will they be able to go home again?

Why are people upset that they want to come here?

How does America currently deal with refugees?

You can also use the checklist below to generate ideas.

Who?

- Who is involved in or affected by my topic?
- Who is my topic about?

What?

- What is the main issue surrounding my topic?
- What about my topic interests me or should interest other people?
- What are the stakes?

When?

- What is the time frame of my topic?
- Is it a current event or a historical event?
- Is it something happening now that will be more of an issue in the future?

Where?

- What geographical area is affected by my topic or where is my topic taking place?
- How is place an important factor in the discussion?

Why?

- Why is my topic worth discussing or researching?
- What are the motives or causes behind my topic?
- Why is the issue happening?

How?

- How are the issues in my topic occurring?
- How are those issues affecting something beyond my topic?

- How can the issues be addressed?
- How do I learn from this?

Incorporating Research

Once you have chosen the topic you want to explore, you will need to learn as much as you can about the ideas you want to write about. Researching your topic will help you learn about the most dominant thoughts surrounding it and allow you to add to that conversation with your own ideas.

The goal of academic research is to locate credible information that can be used to support your claim. Using research to explore the right sources has a number of advantages:

- Strengthens your opinion about a topic by supporting it with fact, details, and evidence
- Offers powerful anecdotes, or long examples told as stories, to highlight your main arguments
- Adds validity to your writing by linking your own claims to experts within your field of study
- Provides timely and relevant information that will advance the education of your audience
- Informs your audience where they can find further information regarding your topic

Read and evaluate the following paragraphs. Which sounds more convincing? If you were trying to make a case against eating celery, which paragraph would you use in your own writing? Why?

Paragraph 1

Perhaps one of humankind's most valued senses is the sense of taste. This sense helps to weed out those foods that humans don't enjoy. At the top of this list is the celery stalk. Celery is disliked by many people, in many parts of the country, so it shouldn't be any real surprise to hear someone complain about the taste.

Paragraph 2

According to a recent study conducted at Yale University, "The most valued human sense is the sense of taste." This sense weeds out those foods that humans don't enjoy. At the top of this list is the celery stalk. According to esteemed researcher Kenneth Braymer, celery has the "lowest success rate in initial taste tests of any food" (96). It shouldn't be any real surprise to hear someone say that "celery tastes like dirt." According to Dr. Kane of the Harvard University Research Team, tree bark actually has more nutritional benefit than a stalk of celery (34).

2b Drafting

Once you have completed pre-writing and researching, it's time to start drafting.

Drafting is when you actually begin writing about your topic and focus on putting your ideas into complete thoughts that form strong paragraphs. You will probably visit this stage of the writing process several times.

In the drafting phase, you need to write an introduction, a thesis statement, a conclusion, and your body paragraphs. You don't have to come up with these sections in that particular order, though, as long as you complete them all. Take a look at the example below:

Introduction: Introduce your topic with an interesting fact, quote, or other item from your research to get the audience interested. Use background information to set up what you will be discussing in the body of the paper. Use your thesis statement to transition into the next body paragraph.

There is a long, troubling history of humans keeping elephants in captivity. From ancient civilizations to present-day circuses and carnivals, these animals have been made to do heavy labor and other things that are unnatural and harmful to them. In the past, people may not have been as aware of how they were mistreating these animals. However, as we have gleaned more knowledge about them, we no longer can justify using elephants for our own petty entertainment; the cost to this amazing species is too great. Elephants in the wild are active up to eighteen hours per day, traveling as many as thirty miles. However, in captivity these animals are confined to small enclosures. This can lead to many physical and psychological problems and drastically reduce quality of life. Elephants should not be kept in captivity because they are an important part of the ecosystem as well as highly intelligent and sensitive creatures.

Some would argue that keeping elephants in captivity is important for educating people about the animals and performing scientific research. Even though many people have stopped supporting circus acts involving elephants, zoos are still extremely popular, and the elephants are often the favorite attraction. People may wonder how children will ever learn about elephants and other exotic animals if they aren't able to see them in zoos.

Body Paragraph 1: This paragraph will develop your argument by using ideas from the introduction and adding research or other sources that challenge what either you or other researchers are writing about your topic. This is also called using a counter-argument.

Body Paragraph 2: The final body paragraph is where you will support your thesis statement either in conjunction with or in spite of your research. Let your audience know what conclusions you have drawn based on your assessment of the topic and its surrounding research paired with your personal viewpoint.

Even though having elephants in zoos does allow millions of people to come in close contact with them and perhaps gain a greater appreciation for them, it is a detriment to the animals themselves. It's hypocritical to claim that having elephants in captivity allows human appreciation of them to grow if the animal's life is unnatural at best and tortured at worst. With our country's level of scientific field research, recording equipment, and dedicated researchers who can access information about these animals in their natural habitat, we have no excuse to continue to have so many elephants in captivity.

> Learning about and appreciating animals is important, and it is awesome to be able to see elephants up close and personal. However, we have to consider the cost. It's not just the price of a ticket, it's the life of an elephant that yearns to roam free, not undergo grueling training and discipline to put on a show. So that elephants can continue to exist as nature intended, we need to have empathy for these extremely intelligent and magnificent animals and sacrifice our own selfish desires to be close to them. Otherwise, we have accomplished the opposite of appreciation.

Conclusion: In the conclusion, avoid re-stating everything from the previous paragraphs. Instead, share ideas for how conversations on your topics may continue and perhaps present other questions to be further explored by you and other researchers. You can also leave your audience with a call to action or a compelling question.

If it helps you, try creating boxes for each part of your essay and writing in them. You can always rearrange what you've written during the next step of the writing process.

2c Revising

A good revision process does not assume that your first draft is the best version. Instead, it enables you to see your writing with fresh eyes. Revision will probably lead you to move, delete, or add entire paragraphs; expand or narrow points; or completely rewrite awkward or confusing passages. Revising your work involves two main areas: focus and development.

- A focused text clearly communicates and supports your main idea. It uses every paragraph to support and expand your thesis statement.

- A developed text presents information effectively and includes many details to support the thesis statement.

One of the best ways to revise a paper is to read it out loud. This will help you hear your tone, check for wording, and understand how your paper sounds to your audience.

When revising for **thesis, focus**, and **style**, here are some questions to ask yourself:

- Is my thesis clear, narrow, and arguable?

- Is my thesis stated explicitly?
- Does the reader have adequate information for understanding my thesis?
- Are all of the main ideas relevant to the thesis?
- Are all of the supporting details relevant to the main ideas?
- Have I chosen a tone that fits the purpose and audience?
- Does my essay maintain a consistent tone?
- Are all unfamiliar terms defined?

When revising for **structure** and **organization**, here are some questions to ask yourself:

- Does my essay develop in a logical progression?
- Have I arranged paragraphs intentionally?
- Does each paragraph develop and maintain a clear main idea?
- Does the introduction hook the reader?
- Does the conclusion summarize well and tie ideas together?
- Does each paragraph have a clear connection to the thesis?
- Does each paragraph use transitions?

2d Editing

After you have written and revised several drafts, it's time to edit your draft. During revision, you focused mostly on ideas, evidence, and organization; during editing, you'll focus on sentence-level edits for grammar and style.

At this stage, it's a good idea to print your paper using double-spaced text so that you can make editing marks throughout.

As you edit, consider these areas of focus:

- Commas and other punctuation
- Spelling and capitalization
- Abbreviations, italics, underlining

- Sentence structure and clarity
- Usage of words and phrases
- Research style guidelines (MLA, APA, CMS, CSE, etc.)

Here's an example:

Unedited:

Religious freedom is a important part of the foundation of are nation. However some people seem to be confused about whom is actually allowed to be free It is true that we are a predomiantly Christian country but that does'nt mean that we shouldn't except other religions as equal. This country was founded so people could excape religions persecution not be subjected too it. Its important that we don't use religion to divide a nation built on acceptance of varied beliefs.

Edited:

Religious freedom is a *n* important part of the foundation of ~~are~~ *our* nation. However, some people seem to be confused about ~~whom~~ *who* is actually allowed to be free. It is true that we are a ~~predomiantly~~ *predominantly* Christian country, but that ~~does'nt~~ *doesn't* mean that we shouldn't ~~except~~ *accept* other religions as equal. This country was founded so people could ~~excape religions~~ *escape religious* persecution, not *so they could be* subjected to it. ~~Its~~ *It's* important that we don't use religion ~~too~~ *to* divide a nation built on acceptance of

varied beliefs.

No matter how you edit your writing, it's a good idea to re-read it several times, focusing on a different area each time.

The Final Draft

Before submitting, publishing, or posting a final draft, you should allow time for some finishing touches. You'll want to make sure that you covered all of your bases during the revision and editing processes.

You will not likely reach a final draft until you've worked through multiple revisions and edits. This is particularly true for longer assignments like research papers.

At this stage, you should complete an evaluation of your paper, marking it up with comments about what you're doing well and what—if anything—could still use some work.

In combination, the revision and editing processes should account for the (applicable) items in each of the following areas.

You can use these items as direction as you evaluate your paper. For example, you might highlight a sentence that uses a lot of effective word variety, while the one that follows is a little too wordy and unclear. Mark up the paper with specific comments about each item you locate.

Organization
Introduction
Thesis Statement
Topic Sentence
Supporting Details
Paragraph Structure
Transition
Conclusion

Agreement
Subject-Verb Agreement
Pronoun-Antecedent Agreement
Pronoun Reference
Pronoun Case
Tense Consistency
Consistency in Person

Logical Fallacy
Evidence
Bias
Relevance

Punctuation
Comma
Colon
Semicolon
Apostrophe
Quotation Marks

Word Choice
Word Variety
Clarity of Word Choice
Awkward Word Choice
Word Meaning
Description
Repetition
Wordy Sentence
Tone
Inclusive/Exclusive
 Language

Sentence Construction
Sentence Fragment
Comma Splice
Run-on Sentence
Word Groups
Misplaced Modifier
Dangling Modifier
Parallelism
Subordination
Coordination
Passive Voice
Active Voice
Sentence Clarity

Mechanics
Spelling
Capitalization
Abbreviations
 Italics

Research
Source Credibility
Citations
Quoting a Source
Paraphrasing a Source
Summarizing a Source
MLA Formatting
APA Formatting
CMS Formatting
 CSE Formatting

Argumentation Strategies
Ethos
Logos
Pathos

2e Reflecting

After completing your final draft, take some time to reflect on the work you've done. Writing can be a long journey, so look over your work with pride and consider what you've learned. The following checklist can provide you with some focus when thinking about your work:

Reflection Checklist

- Reflect on your findings as you evaluated your final draft. In what areas were the greatest strengths and weaknesses of this paper? If your paper was reviewed and/or graded by your instructor, did s/he point out strengths and weaknesses similar to those you determined?

- Reflect on the steps of the writing process that were most helpful. Did these steps help you to write with more purpose than you have in the past?

- Reflect on your purpose and/or thesis and how it evolved through the writing process. Did you answer some of the questions you had at the beginning of the process? Did you support your thesis statement with strong sources and make an impact on your audience?

- Reflect on your writing assignment and how you met those requirements in your work. Did you follow instructions and fulfill the assignment? Did you address a relevant topic in an interesting and well-informed way?

- Reflect on how your ideas and your unique perspective can make a difference. Did you learn something through this process? Do you feel confident as you move forward to new writing assignments?

- Reflect on what you learned not only through your research but also through the process of reading, researching, and entering a larger conversation. Did you find scholarly research that really supported your arguments? Do you feel that you would be welcomed into conversations on your topic?

Below is a sample reflection paragraph that a student might complete during the reflection phase:

After spending weeks on my research project exploring unfair labor practices in the United States, I feel that I've gained a lot of knowledge about these goings-on. I had no idea that so many individuals were being exploited to work at incredibly low wages just so companies can mass-produce their products!

Because of how easy it was for me to find sources that discuss this corruption, it became clear to me that many people all over the country are fighting to end this battle. Many labor unions, in particular, work hard to support workers' rights. However, it isn't always enough to make a real change for everyone, and not all employees have access to this sort of support system.

Although it took a lot of time, I was able to fulfill the requirements of this assignment because I chose a topic that I found interesting. It definitely helped to start with some pre-writing exercises to figure out my focus; initially I thought I'd be researching and comparing various conditions of miners across multiple countries. Though I was somewhat interested in that topic, the one I settled on suited me more.

The best thing I learned from this process is that there is something we can do to help. I found a number of non-profits and government organizations whose missions are to end unfair labor practices and to restore balance in the lower and middle classes. I plan to reach out to one local group later this week!

Exercise

Edit the below paragraph, focusing on punctuation and spelling. There are twenty errors.

When your trying to decide on your career it is important to consider what you're strangths and weaknesses are. Consider your hobbies your extracurricular activities and the things you truly enjoy doing If youre still having trouble figuring it out you can talk to a counsilor at your school or take an online test to determine your top skill sets. Its ok to not know, right away what you are going to do when you finish school but it is important to try to focus as early as possible You don't want to waste alot of time on thinges that wont end up mattering to you, later in life. Talk to youre counselor and get some guidance. Its your future!

Chapter 3

Common Essay Components

Academic essays ask you, the writer, to examine your thoughts and ideas on a particular topic. College instructors will expect you to research, analyze, synthesize, and arrange information in a logical order. Even if the essay is not a research paper, your ideas should be logical and constructed into a focused piece of writing.

You may have learned early on that a typical essay includes five paragraphs, but this is not always the case. Your instructor may expect more, or it may take more than three body paragraphs to support your argument. Unless you are told to meet a certain length requirement, the paragraphs you include should be the number needed to effectively meet your writing goals.

Though your writing guidelines will vary by task and course, they will usually follow this same common format:

1. The introduction paragraph
2. The thesis or purpose statement
3. The body paragraphs
4. The conclusion paragraph

The **introduction** sets the context or background for your argument. It also introduces the content of the essay, presents your thesis or purpose statement, and might hint at how your essay will be organized.

The **body** of the essay is typically made up of at least two paragraphs. Each paragraph contains a topic sentence that presents the central idea; this idea supports the thesis or purpose statement. You should also include developing sentences that further explain the topic as well as examples or evidence that support it further.

The **conclusion** restates the thesis, summarizes the points provided in the body paragraphs, and/or prompts the audience to take action based upon a compelling anecdote, statistic, or call to action.

3a Introductions

The first paragraph of an academic essay is always the introduction. The introduction serves three main purposes, and often proceeds in the order as it's listed below:

1. It hooks the audience's attention
2. It introduces the purpose of your essay by presenting background information
3. It states the thesis of your essay

Exercise

Identify the three parts of an introduction in the following paragraph by writing "hook", "background information", or "thesis statement" next to the example sentence.

Life can be very dull for the person who has no interest in helping others. _____

On the other hand, those who volunteer can get acquainted with interesting people, travel to faraway places, or find the pathway to an exciting career. _____

Developing relationships, gaining travel experience, and learning new skills are three reasons why college students should be required to participate in a volunteer program.

_____

Hooking Your Audience

Obtaining the reader's attention is sometimes referred to as the "hook" because its purpose is to compel your reader to keep reading about your topic. Below are some common ways to tackle this:

- Provide an applicable anecdote or example
- Deliver a strong, relevant quote
- Use a proclamation
- Ask an original, thought-provoking question

You can also use a combination of these methods. However you choose to start your introduction, it must be relevant to your topic. Consider this example:

"Where are they taking that young woman?" I wondered. I was sitting at a bus stop in a village in central Europe. A young man with a dark, menacing look was smoking a cigarette while leaning against a big, black luxury car. Soon, a young woman, maybe sixteen or seventeen years old, was walking toward me with a man who seemed to be guiding her along. As I wondered about what I had seen, it occurred to me. By the time I jerked my head back around, the car was gone. I have tried to rebuild the image of her walking toward me and to see her face in my memory. She wasn't smiling, but was she fearful? Was she a victim of human trafficking? Since I witnessed this experience, I have learned of the prevalence of human trafficking, and not just in Europe. According to the International Labor Organization, 4.5 million adults and children are exploited globally. Pushing for strong anti-trafficking laws and advocating for the education of women are ways to combat human trafficking.

> The example begins with both a quote and a quotation, then recounts an anecdote to get the reader's attention.

Getting to the Point

Your hook is related to the topic of your essay, but it is not enough on its own. After you get your reader's attention, introduce background information.

In the following example, the author hooks the reader by sharing a personal anecdote, then introduces the topic: how Americans should change lawn care.

It's paradise! That was my first thought as I walked into what was about to be my home for the next two years. Grape vines flourished overhead to create a canopy against the hot sun. Roses and lilies were blooming so thickly that they created a wall in front of a huge garden abounding with peppers, tomatoes, squash, okra, herbs, and other vegetables I would learn about later. One side of the garden was lined with fig and walnut trees, and peach trees dotted the garden perimeter. I was in Bulgaria to teach English, but Bulgarians taught me so much more than I taught them.

How is it that Americans have become obsessed with weed-free lawns and ornamental trees? Doesn't it make sense to use our land, no matter how little of it we have, to grow produce? Raising our own produce guarantees that it is fresh and cheaper to consume. In addition, by turning our yards into vegetable gardens, we would no longer need to spray harmful chemicals on the lawn to keep it green and weed-free. Americans should revolutionize lawn care and turn yards into food-producing gardens in order to limit exposure to harmful chemicals and be more economical.

3b Thesis and Purpose Statements

A **thesis statement** is a 1-2 sentence statement that sums up the entire argument of your paper. It is a preview of what your essay is about and how you are going to make that argument. An effective thesis makes a clear, specific, and definable claim. Finally, the thesis statement organizes the structure of your essay.

A thesis statement is not a question or a list. It should not be easily answered with a simple "yes" or "no."

The thesis statement has two main parts:

1. What you plan to argue
2. How you plan to support your argument

Take a look at the thesis statement from the previous paragraph:

> Americans should revolutionize lawn care and turn yards into food-producing gardens in order to limit exposure to harmful chemicals and be more economical.

After reading this, the audience knows exactly *what* the author is going to be writing about: benefits of changing lawn care practices. The reader also knows *how* the author is going to support her claim: by limiting exposure to harmful chemicals and being more economical. Each of these supports will be discussed in its own body paragraph.

You may write, re-write, and refine your thesis statement several times before it captures the essence of your essay and acknowledges the focus of your writing task.

Purpose statements function similarly to thesis statements but are used for different purposes. The purpose statement tells the audience exactly what main points will be covered in a paper and is typically used more in business writing and research reports. Your instructor should provide guidelines on whether to use a thesis statement or a purpose statement in your writing.

Below is an example of a purpose statement:

> This report will describe the goal of the eye-tracking experiment, the results, and the implications for further neurological study.

Exercise

Highlight or underline the thesis statement in the following introduction, then answer the question below.

Bakers need their massive stand-alone mixers, cooks demand a shiny pot or pan for every conceivable use, and chefs want utensils that get the job done, but some kitchen gadgets are a waste of space. Consider the electric can opener. It takes up counter space. It makes a lot of noise. It is also a waste of energy. How hard is it to use a mechanical opener, after all? The electric can opener is one appliance home kitchens can do without.

How is the author going to support this claim?

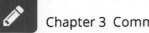

3c Effective Body Paragraphs

Topic Sentences and Supporting Details

The body paragraphs of an academic essay work together to support your thesis statement. Each paragraph should include a **topic sentence** that explains what the paragraph will be about. After your topic sentence is listed, develop the paragraph by using **supporting details** and evidence.

Read the following paragraph. Notice how the topic sentence functions by introducing an idea. This idea is followed by evidence and support.

> Even more comforting for the elderly is the familiarity of personal space. Many seniors have spent their adult lives buying or building a home. Being relegated to a nursing home or assisted care facility is disruptive and often triggers depression and despondency. For patients with life-threatening illnesses, home care options are overwhelmingly preferred. As a matter of fact, the National Hospice and Palliative Care Organization claims "90 percent of Americans prefer to spend their final time at home. If they don't express this, however, they are more likely to die in a facility instead" (4).

In this example, the author explores reasons to support her topic sentence by citing several convincing arguments and a statistic from a credible source.

Transitions

Using transitions helps your audience to naturally follow along with your ideas. Transitions establish relationships between these ideas and give clues about what to expect. The first (and sometimes last) words of a paragraph are crucial to guide your reader through each point in your argument.

Below is a list of common transitional words and phrases:

Although	In conclusion
As we all know	In contrast
As you can see	In general
At the same time	It's evident that
Because of	Obviously
Clearly	On the contrary
Conversely	On the other hand
Even though	Similarly
Finally	Therefore
First	To sum up
Furthermore	Whereas
Given that	While some will argue that
However	
In addition	While this is true
	You may be aware

Within your body paragraphs, you might use transitions for several purposes. Review the examples below:

To shift from one supporting detail to the next

"Dr. Connor's argument is further reinforced by the results of this recent study from …"

To draw contrasts between what is and what might be

"Although current monthly growth is estimated at 15%, we can improve this by …"

To elaborate upon supporting details

"In fact, these statistics are confirmed in a familiar local scenario …"

To introduce support sources

"One nationally renowned expert indicates …"

To acknowledge opposition

"Some may suggest these statistics are skewed, but ..."

You will also likely use transitional sentences that connect your paragraphs and bridge ideas presented in each. These sentences work in the same way that transitional words and phrases do: as connectors between your main points.

Read the paragraph below. Consider the ways in which the last sentence could serve as a transition into a proceeding paragraph.

> There remains a long history of corrupt politicians across countries and continents. Whether it's a monarch, autocratic system, or a democracy, corruption often follows power. Unfortunately, those who pay for this most are low and middle-class citizens. Often, while the interest of these individuals is at the forefront of political messages, the actions of politicians speak otherwise. One major reason for this is the relationships that many big businesses and banks have with politicians. These big companies frequently donate large sums of money to support campaigns for politicians who they feel will best serve their interest. Although some politicians are corrupt, there are others who are well-intentioned and want to embody a voice for the people.

After reading this excerpt, what do you think might be the topic of the next paragraph?

Organizing your Paragraphs

Once you are ready to begin drafting these body paragraphs, try using a graphic organizer to arrange your ideas. A graphic organizer is a visual skeleton on which to build your essay. It may be helpful to use this visual aid before you start writing.

In the following organizer, be sure to fill in your thesis statement first so you can reference it as a guide for developing your ideas. If your focus begins to shift, adjust your ideas or adjust your thesis.

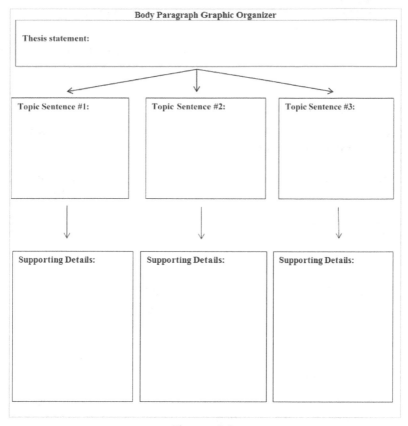

Figure 1.3

3d Conclusions

Purposes of a Conclusion

While the introduction of an essay gets the reader's attention and develops background information needed to present the thesis, the conclusion lets the reader know the essay is coming to an end by restating the thesis and re-connecting it to the main points from the body of the essay.

Instructors may vary on how much information they want in a conclusion, but most agree that the conclusion should do the following things:

- Signal to the reader that you have finished supporting your thesis

- Restate the thesis by using different words to relay the same meaning
- Summarize the points made and/or present a final impression or lasting thought

Conclusion Strategies

Consider the thesis below on the ways in which Edgar Allan Poe's life affected his writing:

> Edgar Allan Poe is known as the father of gothic literature, which is unsurprising since he was exposed early and often to death, disease, and depression.

In your conclusion, how can you say the same thing using different language? Here is an example:

> Because of Poe's tragic upbringing and the deaths of those closest to him, he was able to develop dark and horrifying literature: the trademark of the gothic genre.

Similar to the hook in the introduction, a quote in the conclusion might be appropriate to impact readers:

> As Benjamin Franklin once said, "Justice will not be served until those who are unaffected are as outraged as those who are."

Add a thought that prompts the audience to take action concerning your topic:

> Show your outrage by supporting local efforts to combat these dictatorial curfew laws.

Below is an example of a final conclusion that utilizes several of these strategies:

> As Lenny admires multiple members in her family, she is also forced to watch them shift loyalties, change behaviors, or, most commonly, submit to the demands of those in power. For many children, growing up in a violent war zone has a lasting impact on who they are and what becomes of them. And they are not able to forget or leave it behind. These experiences will always be scars in their memories and imprints on their hearts. It is the child's experience that highlights the true tragedy: a questionable future, an empty present, and, someday, a confused sense of the past. Is this what we want for our children?

First, the author sums up the actions of the main characters.

Then, the author broadens the conclusion to reach a wider audience.

The author ends with a question, leaving the readers to think more about the topic.

Ultimately, the conclusion is *not* the place to add new information. Instead, it is your last chance to persuade your reader to adopt a belief or take an action. It's the place to be direct about your essay's ultimate message.

3e Sample Essay and Organizer

When developing a full essay, try using a graphic organizer like the following one. This document can help you brainstorm and outline your entire essay.

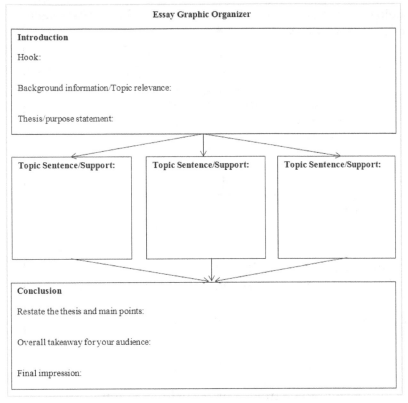

Figure 1.4

Read the following student writing that includes all the common essay components. Where is the thesis statement? How is the thesis restated in the conclusion? Notice how the body paragraphs utilize support for the thesis. Finally, what final impression does the reader leave with you?

This thesis alerts the reader that the essay will describe diverse Mediterranean cruise ports.

For travelers planning the trip of a lifetime, it can be hard to choose the perfect vacation. Some destinations promise relaxation and amenities; others guarantee cultural immersion. A Mediterranean cruise offers a combination of these experiences; it provides luxury accommodations on a ship that travels to a different site almost every day. Each Mediterranean port presents visitors with an opportunity to experience a unique, beautiful, and historic location.

A stop on many Mediterranean cruises is the city of Athens, a modern metropolis abundant with striking monuments from ancient civilizations. The city is just a short metro or taxi ride from the port of Piraeus. History lovers can spend a morning exploring the Acropolis, which includes the ruins of the Parthenon and the theatre of Dionysus; visitors can also enjoy breathtaking panoramic views of the city and surrounding countryside. At the foot of the monument, local shops and restaurants stand just outside the ancient agora, or marketplace, which travelers can explore on foot. Perhaps more than in any other Mediterranean port, past and present are visibly and inseparably intertwined in Athens.

Another common cruise port is the Greek island of Santorini, which is as beautiful as it is in postcards but even more exciting to visit. To get from the cruise ship to the island, visitors have the option of taking a gondola ride with soaring views, a rustic mule ride, or a rugged switchback hike up the side of an extinct volcano. At the top of the cliff, the port town of Skala boasts numerous shops and restaurants. For an afternoon of sand and surf, guests can travel to one of Santorini's famous red or black sand beaches. To experience Santorini at its very finest, visitors can travel by bus to Oia, the famous blue and white town built high above the sea, where they can enjoy al fresco dining overlooking the rooftops, meet local artisans, and experience a typical day on the island.

The details of this paragraph are organized using spatial organization, moving from what visitors first see when they leave the cruise ship to the town on the far side of the island.

If Santorini is striking because of its beauty, Rhodes is striking because of its diverse architecture and rich history. The stone-cobbled Street of the Knights leads to the impressive Palace of the Grandmaster, a huge medieval castle. Elsewhere on the island, excavation sites feature ruins from ancient civilizations. While the famous bronze Colossus of Rhodes—one of the seven wonders of the ancient world—no longer stands astride the island's harbor, Rhodes continues to boast many marvelous examples of the diverse populations that have inhabited the island since the Stone Age.

This topic sentence includes a topic (Athens) and a controlling idea: "a modern metropolis abundant with

The details in this paragraph support the idea that Athens is both modern and full of history.

This concluding sentence supports the topic sentence of the paragraph by restating the main idea.

This phrase transitions from the previous paragraph and reminds readers of the essay's purpose: to describe Mediterranean cruise ports.

This sentence uses a point of contrast to create a transition from the previous paragraph.

The first two sentences of the conclusion restate the essay's purpose and support the idea that a Mediterranean cruise combines culture and luxury.

Mykonos, Crete, Sicily, Rome, Venice, the list of incredible places tourists can visit in a single Mediterranean cruise goes on. Each port promises a new cultural experience; each night aboard the ship ensures fine dining, nightlife, and a new destination in the morning. A Mediterranean cruise just might be the perfect vacation for the adventurous traveler.

Chapter 4

Organizational Patterns

Organizational patterns give your writing order and structure. Using an organizational pattern has two benefits. First, as an author, using an organizational pattern will help you keep your thoughts focused and on-track. Second, an organized piece of writing will be easy for your audience to understand.

There are six common organizational patterns:

Cause and Effect	Order of Importance
Chronological	Spatial
Compare and Contrast	Topical

4a Cause and Effect

A piece of writing that uses the **cause and effect** organizational pattern discusses the causes and/or effects of a topic. Cause and effect is a common pattern in informative or persuasive writing. Use the following signal words and phrases to show the *why* or *how* of your topic:

as a result	due to	since
because	effect	reason
cause	therefore	

Cause and Effect Paragraphs

A paragraph using the cause and effect pattern usually discusses each of a topic's causes or effects in just a few sentences. The outline of a cause and effect paragraph about Hurricane Katrina might look something like this

Topic Sentence	Hurricane Katrina had three major effects on the United States.
Effect 1	Billions of dollars in property damage
Effect 2	Greater awareness of the need for natural disaster preparations

Effect 3	Personal loss for hundreds of people
Concluding Sentence	Property damage, awareness of natural disaster preparation, and personal loss were three major effects of Hurricane Katrina.

Exercise

Fill in the paragraph outline below with causes and a concluding sentence based on the information in the topic sentence.

Topic Sentence: The sales assistant was half an hour late to work this morning.

Cause 1:

Cause 2:

Cause 3:

Concluding Sentence:

Cause and Effect Essays

Using the cause and effect pattern in an essay is more complex than in a paragraph. Since essays tend to be several pages long, there is more room to discuss a topic's causes and effects in more detail. The outline of a cause and effect essay might look something like this:

Introductory Paragraph

Body Paragraph	Effect 1
Body Paragraph	Effect 2
Body Paragraph	Effect 3

Concluding Paragraph

Take a look at this example essay written using a cause and effect organizational pattern.

In 1793, revolutionary France's National Convention established a new calendar that made weeks ten days long, rearranged the months, celebrated new festivals, and changed the year from 1793 to Year 1 of the Revolution. While the Convention ruled, all religion—especially Catholicism—was banned and replaced with the reason and philosophy of the Enlightenment. Consequently, the new calendar was meant to replace the Gregorian calendar used by the Roman Catholic Church. This dramatic change had a negative effect on the attitudes and lives of non-political citizens and a positive effect on local politicians and the National Convention.

> The introductory paragraph ends with a thesis statement that provides the general structure of the essay. The audience can expect the body paragraphs to discuss the following:
> 1. Negative effect
> 2. Positive effect
> 3. Positive effect.

The new calendar had a negative effect on those who did not actively participate in the revolutionary government. Clergyman Abbé Sieyés responded to the proposal of a new calendar by saying that tradition was too strong to be overcome. He claimed that Catholicism had been practiced too long in France, and many other European countries, to be eradicated. According to Sieyés, old habits and customs are not easily prevailed over. Farmers from Étampes, a few miles away from the turbulence of central Paris, wrote to the National Convention in 1794 to state their complaints about the new calendar. They said that nine days of hard manual labor was too much strain. They proposed that Catholic practices were good because they encouraged rest from the distractions of everyday life.

The Gregorian calendar being replaced by the revolutionary calendar had a positive effect on local governments. Picardy, a local government official in the town of Steenwerck, wrote to his superiors about the offensive lack of celebration during the new holidays celebrating reason and philosophy. He also complained that instead of symbols representing liberty, equality, and fraternity, traditional Catholic items were still being displayed. Local government officials supported displacing the Gregorian calendar with the new calendar because it reinforced the power they had gained after the fall of the noble ruling class.

> Each paragraph begins with a topic sentence. However, this writer might want to include better transitions.

This essay uses the signal word *effect* several times.

Finally, the new calendar also had a positive <u>effect</u> on the National Convention. The head of the calendar reform committee, Gilbert Romme, spoke before the National Convention and declared the Gregorian calendar to be a symbol of ignorance. He also equated the old calendar with the French royalty that the Revolution had sought to eliminate. Attempting to create a new calendar strengthened the National Convention's revolutionary ideals and its temporary control over France.

The concluding paragraph summarizes and explains the main points of the essay.

The French Revolutionary calendar had a negative effect on the attitudes and lives of many people in France who were not politically involved, including the clergy and the working class. These groups had close ties to the Catholic Church and the Gregorian calendar. However, it had a positive effect on the power of the local governments and the National Convention. This is because the calendar emphasized the Enlightenment ideals that contributed to the French Revolution.

4b Chronological

Chronological writing shares ideas or events in the order that they happened. Informative and entertaining writing is often organized chronologically. Signal words and phrases that indicate time are associated with a chronological pattern:

after	before	then
afterward	next	
at last	since	

Chronological Paragraphs

A paragraph that uses a chronological organizational pattern could be structured like this:

Topic Sentence	Three things contributed to my most embarrassing moment.
Event 1	I tripped on the stairs
Event 2	I dropped my phone
Event 3	The phone fell on my principal's head

Concluding Sentence	Tripping, dropping my phone, and injuring my principal were the three things that happened to create my most embarrassing moment.

Chronological Essays

Because essays contain multiple paragraphs, a chronological essay could discuss the events of multiple topics, or just spend more time discussing each event in-depth. The outline of a chronological essay might look something like this:

Introductory Paragraph

Body Paragraph   Period of Time 1

Body Paragraph   Period of Time 2

Body Paragraph   Period of Time 3

Concluding Paragraph

Take a look at this example essay written using a chronological organizational pattern.

> From the late 1800s to the mid-1900s, European perceptions of the role of sports changed over time. The Victorian era emphasized the role of sports in morality and character building. After the Victorian era, during WWI, sports were related to war. As the Second World War began, the role of sports was to build physical strength in both men and women.
>
> From 1863 to approximately 1910, sports were seen not only as physically but also morally beneficial. This was the Victorian era, a time associated with ultra-conservative thinking and practices. It was during this time that Robert Baden-Powell founded the Boy Scouts, known today for teaching survival skills and personal integrity. Baden-Powell wrote about the positive moral effect of participating in sports. He claimed that it trained boys for adult life by teaching unselfishness and "a good temper."

This essay's main points are divided into three separate statements. A single, strong thesis statement would improve the introduction.

The beginning of each paragraph indicates a progression through time.

As the Victorian era ended, World War I began in 1914. In the years and months leading up to it, the perception of sports became much more warlike. An article by Mark Berner in the *Berlin Soccer, Track and Field Journal* describes the Olympics as "war, a real war." The article also implies that a country's military rank was directly related to the performance of its athletes. A British military recruitment poster combined images of rowing and cricket with the heading "The Game of War." The poster encouraged young men to enlist in the army and used the idea of war as being the ultimate sport. Paris too adopted the aggressive view of athletic games. The *Paris Encyclopedia of Sports*—published several years after WWI ended—described "the young sportsman" as winning victories on the field and thwarting his opponents.

In the years between the end of the First World War and the beginning of the second, the role of sports changed again. Physical strength became the primary goal of sports and other physical activity. Nikolai Semashko, a doctor and Commissar of Health of Soviet Russia, wrote about the healthful effects of nature and exercise. Additionally, as the women's rights movement gained steam, it became more acceptable for men and women to exercise in the same way. Alice Profe, a German physician, argued that women did not need a different set of physical exercises than men to build up strength. Ingeborg Schröder, a Swedish gymnast in the early 1900s, recalls in her memoir how important physical strength was to both men and women.

From the Victorian era to the 1940s, the way Europeans perceived the role of sports changed over time. In the late 1800s and early 1900s, the role of sports was seen as morally strengthening and character building. During WWI, sports became a type of war. In between the Second and First World War, the role of sports expanded to build physical strength and to include women.

4c Compare and Contrast

Compare and contrast writing discusses the similarities and differences between two topics. This organizational pattern can be used in a variety of ways: describing one topic, then the other topic; discussing similarities and differences together;

or explaining all the similarities in one section and all the differences in another. Descriptive and informative essays often use a compare and contrast pattern.

The following words and phrases signal this pattern:

although	just as
as well as	like
however	on the other hand
in contrast	

Compare and Contrast Paragraphs

A paragraph that compares and contrasts sedans and SUVs might look something like this:

Topic Sentence	Sedans and small SUVs are both popular cars, and tend to be less expensive than other types, but they vary when it comes to gas mileage and horsepower.
Similarity 1	Sedans and small SUVs are two of the most popular car types.
Similarity 2	Sedans and small SUVs are usually less expensive than coupes or large SUVs.
Difference 1	Sedans tend to get better gas mileage than small SUVs
Difference 2	Small SUVs usually have more horsepower than sedans.
Concluding Sentence	While sedans and small SUVs are similar in regard to popularity and price, they differ when it comes to fuel efficiency and power.

Compare and Contrast Essays

Essays that use a compare and contrast organizational pattern will usually have entire paragraphs dedicated to a similarity or difference in their topics.

The outline of a compare and contrast essay might look like this:

Introductory Paragraph

Body Paragraph   Subtopic 1
                            Similarities
                            Differences

Body Paragraph   Subtopic 2
                            Similarities
                            Differences

Body Paragraph   Subtopic 3
                            Similarities
                            Differences

Concluding Paragraph

Take a look at this example essay written with a compare and contrast organizational pattern.

Opening an introduction with a question is a good way to grab the audience's attention.

This is the thesis statement. The audience can expect this essay to address the similarities and differences between cats and dogs with three subtopics: feeding, playing, and level of care.

The signal phrase "In contrast" indicates a comparison.

Have you heard of some people being considered a dog person or a cat person? These are ways to describe people who prefer having a dog as a pet as opposed to a cat or vice versa. What are the similarities and differences between owning a dog and owning a cat? Both cats and dogs need their human to feed them and play with them; however, cats and dogs require different levels of care.

Cats should be fed daily, and some people believe that their cats should always have a full bowl of food that they can visit throughout the day. In contrast, most dog owners will not "free feed" their dogs. This is because dogs tend to eat too much unless their portions are carefully monitored by their owners. Many people will allow their pets to eat "people food," which can lead to unhealthy weight gain. Both cats and dogs can run into serious health problems if they are overweight.

Because cats enjoy climbing and hiding, they don't need much room for exercising. Sometimes, at night or early in the morning, you can catch cats chasing things in the air or chasing each other. You can choose to buy them toys to play with, such as feathers that dangle from a string attached to a stick, small balls that make a jingling sound, or a laser pointer. These will keep them occupied for hours. Unlike cats, dogs need a large space to run around freely in, or you will need to take them for walks once or twice a day. Some breeds require more exercise than others, and no dogs should be crated or locked up all day and night with no exercise or movement. Both cats and dogs need playtime with their owners in order to thrive and get enough exercise.

While cats and dogs are both house pets, they require a different level of care. Cats can be left alone for 1-2 days if they have adequate food and water. They require much less care than dogs. Dogs need an owner who can be active and involved. Depending on which animal you like better, what your job is, and how much time you have for care, one might be a better pet than the other. With both pets, remember that they need regular veterinary checkups and medicine.

The conclusion uses the main points of the essay to summarize the overall differences between cats and dogs. It also connects back to the introduction by making suggestions for pet owners.

4d Order of Importance

Writing that uses an order of importance organizational pattern will organize the information from most important to least important or from least important to most important. Putting most important information at the beginning will grab the audience's attention. Putting most important information at the end will help the audience remember it. Using an order of importance organizational pattern works well for persuasive writing. To indicate levels of importance in your writing, use the following signal words and phrases:

best of all	least
finally	most importantly
key	significant
lastly	

Order of Importance Paragraphs

A paragraph organized by order of importance should discuss each point using a few sentences. A paragraph that uses an order of importance organizational pattern might look like this:

Topic Sentence	Our business needs a new payroll system for the following reasons.
Most Important Point	It would prevent paycheck errors
Less Important Point	It would save the company money
Least Important Point	It would be easier to use
Concluding Sentence	Preventing paycheck errors, saving money, and ease of use are three reasons why our business should use a new payroll system.

Exercise

On a scale of 1 to 3 (1 = most important), rank the main points of the following order of importance paragraph outline. They are listed in no particular order.

Topic Sentence: Wild animals should be protected in every country for three reasons.

____ **Point:** Wild animal conservation preserves the balance of ecological environments.

____ **Point:** Wild animals are beautiful and interesting to observe.

____ **Point:** Protecting wild animals would encourage cooperation among many groups of people.

Concluding Sentence: Wild animals should be protected in every country because conservation preserves ecological balance, wild animals are beautiful and interesting, and protecting wild animals would encourage cooperation among groups of people.

Order of Importance Essays

An order of importance essay will spend at least a paragraph on each point. Additionally, the paragraph that describes the most important point will probably be slightly longer than the others. The outline for an essay that has paragraphs organized in order of importance would look like this:

Introductory Paragraph

Body Paragraph	Most Important Point
Body Paragraph	Less Important Point
Body Paragraph	Least Important Point

Concluding Paragraph

The example essay below is organized by order of importance. Notice that it contains two body paragraphs, not three. This is acceptable as long as your essay meets the assignment guidelines.

What is the average class size of the courses you are taking right now? Whether in high school or college, it seems that the number of students per class is increasing. However, there is still only one teacher to instruct the students. This can cause a lot of problems for even the most talented teacher. The best solution is to reduce class size. Reducing class size would mean that students could receive more one-on-one time with the teacher, and they would feel more comfortable with participating in activities or discussions.

Most importantly, reducing class sizes would make it easier for the instructor to give individual attention to each student. For example, one assignment may take students twenty minutes to complete, and if there is a class of forty people, the teacher only has time to spend thirty seconds with each student. If one student is struggling or has a question, the teacher may not have time to help him or her. However, studies show that an increase in student-teacher interaction is related to an increase in academic achievement. Having less students in the class will allow the teacher more time to visit with each and every student.

The thesis statement includes two main benefits of reducing class size: 1. one-on-one time between students and teachers, and 2. increased student participation. Not all essays must have three body paragraphs.

The signal phrase "Most importantly" indicates that this essay will discuss information from most to least importance.

A less significant but still important benefit of reducing class size is that the students will be more likely to participate. Students need to feel comfortable in order to speak up in class. Large classes of unfamiliar faces can be intimidating. This could cause students to be too nervous to ask or answer questions. If students are in small groups and are familiar with their classmates, they are more likely to get involved in activities or discussions.

> In the conclusion, the writer mentions a counter-argument. This demonstrates the writer's awareness of multiple perspectives, and actually strengthens the writer's own argument.

While some people might argue that it is more cost-effective to have more students in the classroom, does it benefit student learning to focus on money rather than the value of the education they are receiving? Reducing class size should be a priority for all schools. The key benefit for students would be more one-on-one attention from instructors. Also, smaller classes would encourage students to participate in discussions and activities. School administrators and teachers can get together and agree on a maximum class size that makes them both happy.

4e   Spatial

Spatial writing describes a topic by its physical characteristics. These descriptions usually follow a logical direction, such as side to side, top to bottom, or inside to outside. A spatial organizational pattern is effective for entertaining or informative writing. Spatial signal words and phrases will indicate location and are often prepositions or prepositional phrases:

above	in front of	outside
across	inside	to the left/right
below	next to	

Spatial Paragraphs

Because paragraphs are short, a spatial paragraph must effectively use a few descriptive sentences to portray a topic. The outline of a paragraph using a spatial organizational pattern might look something like this:

Topic Sentence	My dorm room is small, but it has everything I need.
Physical Characteristic 1	On the left wall are my bed and a small bedside table.
Physical Characteristic 2	In front of the bed, there is a sink, mirror, and tall cabinet.
Physical Characteristic 3	On the right wall, there is a large desk with built-in shelves.
Concluding Sentence	Even though my dorm room is small, it contains what I need to be comfortable.

Spatial Essays

Spatial essays have more room to describe all aspects of a topic. The outline of a spatial essay would probably look like this:

Introductory Paragraph

Body Paragraph	Physical Characteristic 1
Body Paragraph	Physical Characteristic 2
Body Paragraph	Physical Characteristic 3

Concluding Paragraph

Take a look at this essay that uses a spatial organizational pattern.

Ron shuddered as he walked into the silent room, a feeling of nostalgia and displacement creeping through his veins. The smell of must and memory pervaded his senses. "I wish Joanne was here," he told himself as he scanned the contents to his left. The old, circular window was still there, clouded with dust. How many days had he spent in the living room peering through that window, watching in awe and frustration as his brothers chased footballs and girls? For a moment, the old surge of jealousy hit him unexpectedly. He laughed aloud and thought, "It's hard being the youngest."

The description of the house moves through it in a way that parallels the movement of the main character, Ron.

Because spatial essays focus on a topic's physical characteristics, including vivid descriptions is especially effective.

On the right, the doorway to the kitchen loomed in front of Ron, daring him to enter. As he walked through the hallway, passing the rows of framed pictures, his unease turned to fondness, his frown to quiet tears. "How quickly it all went by," he sighed. Walking into the kitchen, he could practically smell the blueberry muffins he'd spent hours baking with his mother. She'd reassured him that one day he and his brothers would become good friends. Though he had never believed her, part of him still appreciated her encouragement. The secret winks and extra helpings of dessert had assured Ron that he was her stealthy favorite. Ron jumped as the faded red curtains swayed with the breeze, and the wind chimes made the sound of home that he'd heard all of his childhood years.

He moved left, to the table, and picked up the last newspaper his father had ever read, and smiled to see the "Job Ads" section circled with red marker. Even in retirement, his father was never content. The memory of his father stayed with him as he walked through the garage door in the corner, his eyes resting on decaying boxes and rusty car parts. He thought of the afternoons he spent as a teenager working with his father to repair the old Ford pick-up. Though the time was seldom spent exchanging words, it was his father's way, and he could hear the clanking of the tools just as vividly as he could smell his mother's blueberry muffins.

Ron lifted the corrugated metal garage door and walked outside. He surveyed the yard, the driveway, and the fence. "The backdrop of my childhood," he thought. He got in his car in the driveway and stared at the house for a few more minutes. Then, he drove home to his own sons. "Alright," he said, "it's time for a game of football. Even you, Ron." And he winked at his youngest son, who lit up as he ran with his brothers to the backyard.

4f Topical

Topical writing discusses pieces of information that are equally important, so it doesn't need to be arranged in a particular order. This is a common organizational pattern because it will fit nearly any topic. Informative or reflective writing will often be organized topically. Because this pattern has no specific structure, signal words and phrases are especially important:

first	main point	to begin
finally	next	
last	second	

Topical Paragraphs

A topical paragraph would dedicate a few sentences to each topic. The outline of a topical paragraph could look something like this:

Topic Sentence	Flavored coffee, green tea, and soda are three of the most commonly consumed beverages in America.
Topic 1	Flavored coffee has become increasingly popular
Topic 2	Green tea is widely consumed for its health benefits
Topic 3	Soda comes in hundreds of flavors
Concluding Sentence	The most commonly consumed beverages in America are flavored coffee, green tea, and soda.

Topical Essays

The outline of an essay using a topical organizational pattern might look like this:

Introductory Paragraph

Body Paragraph	Topic 1
Body Paragraph	Topic 2
Body Paragraph	Topic 3

Concluding Paragraph

Take a look at this essay that uses a topical organizational pattern.

The introduction's thesis statement clearly provides the essay's main points: natural oils, fans, and bacteria are alternative bug repellants. Because this essay uses a topical organizational pattern, these points are equally important.

Backyard barbecues, poolside afternoons, and lawn games are just some of the welcome activities that summer brings. Unfortunately, these opportunities for enjoying the outdoors are often accompanied by an uninvited guest: the mosquito. Most active early in the morning and late in the afternoon, the mosquito can ruin a perfect summer day with its annoying buzz and itchy bites. Although DEET-based sprays are perhaps most widely available, they can have negative health and environmental effects. Three ways to repel mosquitos, without using DEET, are natural oils, fans, and bacteria.

Some natural oils, particularly those from lemon-scented plants, have been found to keep mosquitoes at bay. Citronella oil is an essential oil made from lemongrass, and can be an effective insect repellant. Eucalyptus oil, made from the leaves of eucalyptus plants, is another popular, natural insecticide. Using a combination of several essential oils will create a stronger bug repellant, whether you make it at home or buy it ready-made. One disadvantage of natural oils is that they require more frequent re-application, usually every thirty to sixty minutes.

A second way to repel mosquitos is to use a fan. Mosquitoes are poor fliers, so setting up a large fan on a deck or patio can help keep them away from a small outdoor area. The air flow will disrupt their flying pattern and discourage them from flying in that area. Fans can serve a double purpose of keeping you cool in the summer heat and keeping away pesky bugs. However, two issues could arise from this method of repelling mosquitos. First, you may not have an electrical outlet outdoors, or it may not be in the right location on your house. Second, long extension cords can become a safety hazard.

Each paragraph includes both the positive and nega-tive aspects of each topic.

A third option for repelling mosquitos without using DEET is to use *Bacillus thuringiensis israelensis* (Bti). Bti is a kind of bacteria that is harmless to humans but destroys mosquito eggs, which are laid in water. Floating discs of Bti can be used in pools and birdbaths, and Bti pellets can be sprinkled in gutters and other places where rainwater collects. This method will not keep away mosquitos that are already bothering you, but it will prevent them from multiplying.

Natural oils, fans, and Bti are three ways to repel mosquitos. These methods are safer and more natural than DEET-based products. When the weather gets warm, try one or a combination of these strategies to keep mosquitos from ruining the fun!

Chapter 5

Writing Across the Curriculum

English instructors usually teach writing because it's is a language-related skill, but writing is an expression of reasoning, so it applies to every discipline.

5a Similarities & Differences in Writing Assignments

All texts can be traced down to one basic starting point: an author has a goal of communicating *something* to *some* audience. From that starting point, different aspects of the writing situation—the assignment details, the complexity of the topic, the target audience, the intended outcome, and the mode of delivery—shape the development of a text.

Common Purposes

Regardless of the course you're writing for, your paper will likely include some combination of these purposes:

- **Writing to Discuss:** exchanging ideas or explaining a situation surrounding a topic
- **Writing to Respond:** reacting to and drawing implications from the main ideas of a text
- **Writing to Summarize:** providing a small, generalized overview of a larger piece of information
- **Writing to Describe:** using vivid details to illustrate a person, place, idea, experience, or event
- **Writing to Argue:** convincing the audience to adopt a belief or take an action
- **Writing to Propose:** providing recommendations for solving a problem
- **Writing to Analyze:** understanding a topic by examining its parts
- **Writing to Evaluate:** judging the strengths and weaknesses of an idea, process, or outcome

What Instructors Expect

No matter the discipline, the components of effective writing almost always include the following criteria:

> ## Writing Checklist
>
> - ✓ Write coherently, clearly, and concisely
> - ✓ Observe the conventions of written language
> - ✓ Analyze, evaluate, interpret data and other field-specific content
> - ✓ Develop theses and purpose statements
> - ✓ Form compelling arguments and support them
> - ✓ Organize ideas strategically
> - ✓ Cite sources appropriately

Course- and Discipline-Specific Factors

Topics and Main Ideas

The **topic** is the general subject of a text. For example, in a literature course, you're likely to explore topics related to themes and characters. In a psychology course, you're more likely to explore topics related to particular theories and experiments.

The **main idea** is the statement or argument that a text communicates about its topic. Main ideas are much more specific than topics, so these are the statements that really shape the development of the writing. For example, imagine that a philosophy professor and a biology professor are both writing articles about the topic of love. Although the topic is the same, the main idea of each respective article is likely very different. Moreover, the philosophical approach probably isn't relevant to the goals of the biology professor's writing.

Focus, Language, and Delivery

Instructors evaluate writing based on a variety of factors. When your English instructor grades your expository essay, s/he is probably focusing on things like word choice, transitions, supporting details, grammar, and spelling.

Your environmental research professor, however, cares much more about getting a concise snapshot of the pollutants you found during your last experiment. She wants to see clear, organized, quality writing, but she places even higher values on things like precision, accuracy, and well-informed conclusions. Visuals like charts and graphs will help her locate this sort of information.

Research Styles

Especially for research assignments, instructors often require students to use a particular research style. A research style guide is a set of standards used for research and scholarly writing within a particular discipline.

- MLA (Modern Language Association)
- APA (American Psychological Association)
- CMS (Chicago Manual of Style)
- CSE (Council of Science Editors)

Each of these style guides lays out its own unique rules for preferred language, formatting, and source integration within a research paper.

The rest of this chapter will provide an overview of writing conventions and assignments for specific subject areas.

5b English, Literature, and Language Studies

Common Writing Purposes in Literary Studies

In literature and other reading- or writing-focused courses, you will encounter various types of writing assignments, including many that are common in other disciplines. In fact, most schools require composition courses that are meant to prepare students for writing across disciplines throughout their college careers.

Reading- and writing-related assignments usually allow— and often encourage—more subjective arguments than do business- or science-related assignments. For this reason, assignments within the humanities are more likely than others to include the following purposes:

- Writing to describe
- Writing to respond
- Writing to discuss

Common Assignments for Literature Courses

Here are two of the most common writing assignments you'll encounter in a literature-specific course:

- Literary or rhetorical analysis
- Book review (may also apply to movie or theatre)

What Literature Instructors Expect

No matter what kind of writing assignment you do in a literature or other English course, instructors will have certain expectations.

Writing Checklist: Literature

- ✅ Strong thesis and development

- ✅ Relevant, meaningful evidence

- ✅ Clear purpose and audience awareness

- ✅ Effective use of style and organization

- ✅ Proper grammar and spelling

Common Research Styles

MLA style is the go-to format for citing sources in most writing assignments within the Humanities.

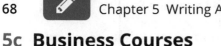

5c Business Courses

Common Writing Purposes in Business Courses

Writing to Persuade

Business is all about selling and promoting. Marketing, advertising, public relations, investor relations, management, and customer interactions all share the goals to increase profit and advance the company's visibility and viability. Persuasion plays a role in every business writing task.

Writing to Analyze

Business progress depends on analysis. There's always a better way to operate, a new market to explore, or a place to trim expenses and add value. Analysis includes close scrutiny of assets and liabilities, areas for improvement, and ways to cut costs.

Common Assignments for Business Courses

In business courses and professional writing, you will often encounter the following writing assignments:

Assignment	Purpose
Cover letter and résumé	Obtain an interview or job
Press release	Inform/promote business or related event
Blog post/social media	Inform/promote business
Memo/email	Inform, share findings, recommend action
Business plan	Make a case for starting a business or request a loan
Marketing plan	Make a case for a new approach or a new campaign
Executive summary	Summarize a longer proposal or plan

Assignment	Purpose
Proposal	Analyze an issue, evaluate options, and recommend action
Feasibility study	Analyze needs, evaluate options, and recommend strategy
Grant writing	Persuade investors to fund or subsidize a business

What Business Instructors Expect

Writing Checklist: Business

- ✅ Focused, concise argument
- ✅ Well-supported claims
- ✅ Evidence including case studies and data
- ✅ Clear organization and transitions
- ✅ Short, parallel subheadings for each section
- ✅ Paragraphs have no more than 250 words
- ✅ Sentences have no more than 35 words

Research Styles for Business Courses

There is no official format for business writing. Instead, format is determined by instructors or the business school. Be sure to ask about the preferred formatting before you begin writing. Some common styles are American Psychological Association (APA), Chicago Manual of Style (CMS), and Modern Literature Association (MLA).

5d History

Common Writing Purposes in History Courses

Writing to Analyze

Taking apart another historian's work and considering its value is an important part of historical research and the process of isolating credible sources of information. Analysis is a key step in demonstrating connections (such as cause and effect) between historical events.

Writing to Evaluate

History students usually spend a lot of time comparing and evaluating the credibility and usefulness of sources. Since there has been so much written about history, from so many different perspectives, it's important to be able to recognize and eliminate biased or unreliable sources.

Common Assignments for History Courses

In history courses, you will often encounter these writing assignments:

Assignment	Purpose
Annotated bibliography	Assess and summarize sources and content
Historiographical survey	Analyze other historians' work
Document analysis	Analyze, discuss, and evaluate a text
Formal essay on assigned text	Critically evaluate and analyze a primary source
Research paper	Provide reliable information, argument, and comparison of sources
Biographical sketch term paper	Research and assess the life and impact of a historical figure

Assignment	Purpose
Autobiographical familial paper	Analyze genealogical research documents

The Annotated Bibliography

In particular, annotated bibliographies are crucial for success in a history course. Annotated bibliographies are more than a list of citations because they also include a short summary and assessment of the usefulness and credibility of each source.

Here's an example of an entry in entry in an annotated bibliography:

> Riekenberg, H.W. (1986). *"The Building of the Hermannsburg – German Immigration to Kansas Territory in the 1870s."* New York: Random House.

This semi-autobiographical account chronicles the influx of German farmers into the Midwest during the late 19th century. It details seven generations of Lutheran dairy farmers, their struggle for survival on the prairie, and the building of small, well-organized townships in the Kansas Territory of the 1870s-1900s. The author includes early photos and describes social gatherings, church architecture, and agricultural statistics—including output, livestock, and inheritance—along with population and local government.

What History Instructors Expect

> ### Writing Checklist: History
>
> ✅ Original ideas, research, and analysis
>
> ✅ Focused interpretation and argumentation
>
> ✅ Well-organized research with primary and secondary sources
>
> ✅ Critical analysis of sources
>
> ✅ Mastery of both factual material and the "big picture"
>
> ✅ Proper documentation/citation format
>
> ✅ Correct grammar and spelling

Common Research Styles for History Courses

The preferred citation style in history courses is Chicago Manual of Style.

5e Psychology

Common Writing Purposes in Psychology Courses

Analysis/Interpretation

In the sciences, testing and presenting results accurately is not enough. Psychologists must interpret the data and recommend a plan of action. This may mean recommending a treatment plan, further testing, or changes in the testing procedure.

Persuasion/Rhetoric

Since data can be interpreted in many ways, the interpretation and recommendation for next steps requires persuasion. Supporting details must be provided for any recommendations. References to other studies and compelling data are key. Recommended treatment plans must be accompanied by careful consideration of side effects, duration, and expected results.

Common Assignments for Psychology Courses

In psychology courses, you will often encounter these writing assignments:

Assignment	Purpose
Position paper	Take a position on a topic; analyze, argue, and defend it with evidence
Research paper	Describe, analyze, and synthesize primary and secondary support sources
Case study	Analyze a human subject and determine a diagnosis and intervention
Psych evaluation	Analyze data from formal assessment and recommend treatment
Lab report	Record details, processes, and results of an experiment
Critique of article	Evaluate a professional academic article based on established criteria
Journal article	Analyze study or research data with thesis and support

What Psychology Instructors Expect

Writing Checklist: Psychology

- ⊘ Logical and well-developed argumentation
- ⊘ Evidence from empirical research and scientific sources
- ⊘ Concise presentation of ideas and arguments

Common Research Styles for Psychology Courses

American Psychological Association (APA) style is required for writing assignments in psychology courses, social sciences, economics, nursing, and some business-related writing.

5f Lab Sciences

Common Writing Purposes in Science Courses

Writing to Summarize, Analyze, Evaluate, and Propose

In lab sciences, testing and presenting results accurately is not enough. Lab science students must interpret data and recommend a plan of action. This may include recommending further testing or research.

Writing to Argue

Since data can be interpreted in many ways, the interpretation and recommendation for next steps requires persuasion. Supporting evidence must be provided for any recommendations. This includes references to other research results with compelling statistics. To perform further research, scientists may need to persuade a committee or department to provide funding.

Common Assignments for Science Courses

In lab science courses, you will often encounter these writing assignments:

Assignment	Purpose
Research paper	Analyze and present a conclusion with reliable support
Case study	Report research, interpret results, provide support, make recommendations
Argument	Defend a position with data and reliable support
Journal article	Defend a new theory based on research
Proposal for research	Analyze and make a case for viability; may involve funding

Assignment	Purpose
Review of article	Evaluate merit of study and conclusions based on prescribed criteria
Lab report	Describe and document procedure and results of experiment or study
Critical evaluation	Analyze and assess research or a study

What Lab-Science Instructors Expect

Writing Checklist: Lab Sciences

- ✓ Demonstrate understanding of the scientific process

- ✓ Present information concisely, with a simple, clear statement of the scientific question

- ✓ Complete description of the methods of study and the results

- ✓ Provide context before introducing new information

- ✓ Use strong, clear transitions, linking backwards and contextualizing forward

Common Research Styles for Science Courses

Some sciences require American Psychological Association (APA) style, while others expect Chicago Manual of Style (CMS).

5g Engineering and Technology

Common Writing Purposes in Engineering and Technology Courses

Writing to Analyze

Engineers often write procedural manuals for installing and upgrading existing machinery and proposals for construction and renovation of plants and utilities. This requires analysis and synthesis as well as step-by-step procedure for changes and cost structure.

Writing to Evaluate

Technical reports detail problems with infrastructure, machinery, and systems. Analysis is required to find the problem source, while evaluation is necessary to find the best solution. Engineers often recommend solutions and describe the procedure for implementing the solution.

Common Assignments for Engineering and Technology Courses

In engineering and technology courses, you will often encounter these writing assignments:

Assignment	Purpose
Technical description	Simplify technical concepts and processes
Technical reports	Analyze and describe a problem, then prescribe a solution
Critique of article	Analyze/evaluate design, conclusions, and sources
Progress report	Provide incremental information on the stages of an ongoing project
Proposal	Assess and define a problem and recommend a solution
Process manual	Simplify a procedure
Journal/conference article	Present findings, including analysis, procedure, and recommendation. Highly structured and regulated submission requirements

What Engineering and Technology Instructors Expect

Writing Checklist: Engineering and Technology

- Interpret figures and diagrams

- Logical thought sequences toward solution of the problem

- Provide a course of action: what do you want readers to do?

- Provide valid evidence to support your claims

- Use standard conventions for presenting figures and appendices

- Use concrete key terms consistently throughout the document

- Identify any terms that readers won't recognize immediately

- Write in complete sentences, not just phrases

Common Research Styles for Engineering and Technology Courses

For engineering courses, refer to Institute of Electrical and Electronics Engineers (IEEE) format specifications. Some technology courses require style and formatting according to the Mayfield Guide. Check the assignment guidelines or course syllabus to determine which is applicable, or ask your instructor for clarification.

Effective Sentences

Chapter 6

Combining Word Groups

When you write, one of your main goals should be to show connections between ideas. Some ideas are equally important to your meaning, while others are less important. The way that you structure a sentence can help establish those relationships and give your writing a smoother flow.

6a Coordination

When two word groups discuss ideas that are closely related, they can be combined using coordination. There are two ways to join word groups with coordination:

- Use a comma + coordinating conjunction
- Use a semicolon

Use a Comma + Coordinating Conjunction

Use a comma and a coordinating conjunction to join two independent clauses. Use the acronym FANBOYS to remember the seven coordinating conjunctions:

F	A	N	B	O	Y	S
For	And	Nor	But	Or	Yet	So

Take a look at these examples that use a comma with a coordinating conjunction:

Marco is a football fanatic, but he likes baseball even better.

It has finally stopped raining, and the sun is shining again.

My boyfriend is allergic to peanuts, so I don't eat them either.

Use a Semicolon

Using a semicolon is another way to combine two independent clauses.

> Marco is a football fanatic; he likes baseball even better.

> It has finally stopped raining; the sun is shining again.

> My boyfriend is allergic to peanuts; I don't eat them either.

Exercise

Practice combining the independent clauses below either with a comma and coordinating conjunction or with a semicolon.

My friend is majoring in nursing. She is constantly studying.

Last night, the temperature dropped. My car's windshield was covered with ice.

Nate wants to see a movie tonight. I want to go to a party.

6b Subordination

Another word for "subordinate" is "dependent." Like coordination, subordination combines word groups that discuss related ideas. However, subordination makes one word group dependent on another word group.

Here's a list of common subordinating conjunctions:

after	despite	since
although	even though	until
as	if	when
because	once	while

At the Beginning of a Sentence

Use a subordinating conjunction to make one sentence dependent on a second sentence.

The power went out.

We used candles for light.

Because the power went out, we used candles for light.

When the dependent word group is at the front of the sentence, it is separated from the other word group by a comma.

Here are a few more examples:

Since it's Friday, everyone in the office is dressed casually.

Even though the event was cancelled, people still showed up.

At the End of a Sentence

When a dependent word group is at the end of a sentence, no comma is needed.

Everyone in the office is dressed casually since it's Friday.

People still showed up even though the event was cancelled.

Exercise

Practice combining two independent clauses below with a subordinating conjunction. When you're finished, each sentence should contain one dependent clause and one independent clause.

The job market is very competitive. I want to apply to a number of positions in my area.

I dislike costume parties. I have to dress up so I can go out to my friend's Halloween party.

Math is my favorite subject in school. I am taking two English courses this semester.

6c Parallelism

In writing, parallelism is used to create balance between two or more related ideas by using similarly-structured words, phrases, or clauses. Parallelism can be used for the following types of sentences:

- Combined word groups
- Lists

Combined Word Groups

You can use coordination or subordination to combine two word groups. However, if the word groups are structured in two different ways, it will be difficult to see the connection between the two pieces of information.

> My sister has a bulldog; a golden retriever is what my brother has.

To make this sentence parallel, one of the independent clauses needs to be changed so that both clauses follow the same basic pattern:

Person	My sister
Action	has
Dog	a bulldog

If the second independent clause is changed to follow this pattern, the sentence will be parallel and the two ideas will be more clearly connected.

> My sister has a bulldog; my brother has a golden retriever.

Here are a few more examples of independent clauses connected with parallelism.

> Take out the trash on Monday; sweep the floors on Tuesday.

> My mom likes to stay up late on her birthday; my dad likes to sleep late on his birthday.

My roommate is majoring in chemistry; my best friend is majoring in journalism.

Lists

Lists are easy to read when each item follows the same parallel structure.

Not Parallel	This afternoon, I want to finish my essay, my car needs to be cleaned out, and buying milk is necessary.
Parallel	This afternoon, I want to finish my essay, clean out my car, and buy milk.
Not Parallel	Sherman Alexie is a talented novelist, he is also a screenwriter, and he has written poetry.
Parallel	Sherman Alexie is a talented novelist, screenwriter, and poet.

In the parallel lists, each item follows the same basic structure, making it much easier to read than the lists that aren't parallel.

Exercise

Re-write the sentence below so that the list items use a parallel structure.

My neighbor's parakeet, the cat that belongs to my grandmother, and my best friend's hamster came to my dog's birthday party.

Chapter 7

Agreement

When two people agree on something, like "mint chocolate chip is the best ice cream flavor," it means that even though they are two different individuals, they are the same when it comes to at least one issue (in this case, ice cream flavors). In effective sentences, your words are different from each other, but they need to agree with each other, or be the same, in certain ways. Agreement needs to happen between two types of words:

- Subjects and verbs
- Pronouns and antecedents

7a Subject-Verb Agreement

The way that subjects and verbs need to agree is in "number." All subjects and verbs are either singular or plural in number. "Singular" means *one*, and "plural" means *many*. Singular subjects are always paired with singular verbs. Take a look at these examples:

My friend writes posts for her blog every week.

The sparrow looks for crumbs on the busy sidewalk.

The update is available to download for free.

Similarly, plural subjects are always paired with plural verbs. Take a look at these examples:

Cars need regular maintenance checks.

Raindrops slide down the car window.

The puppies are three weeks old today.

Notice that the spelling of singular and plural verbs is unexpected. Singular verbs often end in the letter *s*, while plural verbs usually don't. In contrast, singular nouns often don't end in the letter *s*, while plural verbs often do.

Compound Subjects

A compound subject is a subject made up of two nouns or pronouns that are usually joined by a conjunction, like "Bonnie and Clyde." When a sentence contains a compound subject, you must use special guidelines to decide if the subject is singular or plural.

If a compound subject uses the following conjunctions, it's plural and needs a plural verb.

> and
>
> both, and
>
> Marta and John answer questions at the end of each training session.
>
> Both Sokwe the chimpanzee and Fisi the hyena were born in captivity.

If a compound subject uses any of the following conjunctions, use the part of the compound subject that is closest to the verb to decide whether the verb needs to be singular or plural.

> nor
>
> neither, nor
>
> or
>
> either, or
>
> Either the closets or the bathroom needs to be cleaned today.

Closets is plural, but because the other part of the subject, *bathroom*, is singular and closest to the verb, the verb is singular too. Here are a few more examples:

> Neither blueberries nor blackberries are in season right now.
>
> This bus or the next one is always on time.

Indefinite Pronouns

Indefinite pronouns refer to non-specific people or objects. Some indefinite pronouns are always singular or always plural. Others can be singular or plural depending on how they are used in a sentence.

Singular		Plural	Both
anybody	everything	both	all
anyone	nobody	few	any
anything	no one	many	most
each	nothing	several	none
everybody	somebody		some
everyone	someone		
	something		

To decide if the words *all, any, most, none,* or *some* are plural, look at what the indefinite pronoun is referring to.

Singular: All of the cake has already been eaten.

Plural: All of the orders have been filled on time.

Singular: Most of the building has been remodeled.

Plural: Most of the cars are parked.

Distracting Words and Phrases

When words and phrases come between a subject and its verb, it can be difficult to use subject-verb agreement. However, the subject of a sentence will never appear inside a prepositional phrase. A prepositional phrase starts with a preposition and ends with a noun or pronoun.

Subject-Verb Checklist

Use the following steps to find the subject and verb in a complicated sentence.

- ✓ Put parentheses around any prepositional phrases

- ✓ Identify the verb

- ✓ Identify the subject

- ✓ Determine if the subject and verb agree in number

The people in the elevator is stuck between the third and fourth floors.

The people (in the elevator) is stuck (between the third and fourth floors).

The people (in the elevator) is stuck (between the third and fourth floors).

The people (in the elevator) is stuck (between the third and fourth floors).

In this example, the subject and verb do not agree because *people* is plural and *is* is singular. Here is the correct version:

The people in the elevator are stuck between the third and fourth floors.

Inverted Word Order

When a sentence has regular word order, the subject comes before the verb.

The squirrel dashes across the street.

"Inverted" means switched, so sentences with inverted order put the verb before the subject.

Across the street dashes the squirrel.

To find out if a sentence with inverted word order uses subject-verb agreement, use the same steps as you would for a sentence with distracting words or phrases.

Take a look at this example:

Into the store walk three mysterious men.

(Into the store) walk three mysterious men.

(Into the store) walk three mysterious men.

(Into the store) walk three mysterious men.

Exercise

Circle the sentences below that use subject-verb agreement.

The basketball player dribbled the ball easily.

The actors or the producer are attending the event.

Somebody is giving a presentation in class tomorrow.

The cookies on the blue plate in the kitchen is for my niece's birthday.

Around the block moved the large parade.

7b Pronoun-Antecedent Agreement

A pronoun is a word that takes the place of a noun in a sentence. Pronouns are often paired with an antecedent, which is the word that the pronoun renames.

The firefighter put on her helmet.

In this sentence, *her* is a pronoun and *firefighter* is the antecedent. Pronouns and their antecedents must agree, or be the same, in two ways: gender and number. These two categories work together; for example, a pronoun could be "singular, male" or "plural, neutral."

Number

Pronoun number has two categories: singular and plural

Singular	Plural
I, me, my, mine	we, us, our, ours
you, your, yours	you, your, yours
he, him, his	they, them, their, theirs
she, her, hers	
it, its	

The number of a pronoun must agree with the number of its antecedent. Take a look at these examples:

Singular: My tablet needs its screen repaired.

Singular: The candidate shared her opinions during the debate last night.

Plural: My twin cousins celebrate their birthday together.

Plural: Since this family is small, we don't need two cars.

Gender

Pronoun gender has three categories: male, female, and neutral.

Male	Female	Neutral
he, him, his	she, her, hers	I, me, my, mine
		we, us, our, ours
		you, your, yours
		it, its
		they, them, their, theirs

The gender of a pronoun must agree with the gender of its antecedent. Take a look at these examples:

Male: Uncle Ken left his glasses in the car.

Female: The little girl was sitting on her father's shoulders.

Neutral: That tree is losing its leaves already.

If the gender of the antecedent is unknown, there are two options.

Use the term *he or she* or *his or her.*

   An employee should eat his *or* her lunch in the break room.

Make the antecedent plural in number and use a pronoun that is neutral in gender

   Employees should eat their lunches in the break room.

Chapter 8

Modifiers

8a Using Modifiers

Modifiers are words or word groups that add extra information to a sentence. Another word for modifier is *describer* because modifiers describe other words or word groups. Without modifiers, sentences would be less meaningful and clear. Take a look at this example:

With Modifiers: The red-faced man frantically sprinted down the street.

Without Modifiers: The man sprinted down the street.

With Modifiers: The woman leaning nonchalantly against the doorframe observed the crowd.

Without Modifiers: The woman observed the crowd.

Common Types of Modifiers

The most common types of modifiers are adjectives and adverbs.

Seasoned Minnesotans rarely dream of living in a warmer climate.

The dusty shelf hung diagonally above an ancient stove.

However, sometimes phrases and even clauses are also considered modifiers.

As she backed out of the driveway, Bridget realized she'd left her glasses inside.

All of the students on the volleyball team are experienced athletes.

Absolute Modifiers

One more type of modifier is the "absolute" modifier. Absolute modifiers are complete by themselves and don't need words like *very* or *extremely* in front of them.

> The tree in the front yard is ~~completely~~ dead.

Either the tree is dead or it is alive; using the word *completely* incorrectly implies that there are varying degrees of death.

Absolute modifiers also do not make sense in comparisons.

> In Greek mythology, gods like Zeus and Hera are ~~more~~
> immortal ~~than the humans~~ *while humans are not.*

Here are a few more examples of absolute modifiers.

entirely	identical	perfect
eternal	infinite	right
fatal	irrevocable	straight
final	mortal	
finite	opposite	

8b Misplaced and Dangling Modifiers

While modifiers are meant to add meaning and clarity to a sentence, they can end up creating confusion if they're used incorrectly. There are two common modifier errors:

- Misplaced modifiers
- Dangling modifiers

Misplaced Modifiers

A misplaced modifier is too far away from the word it modifies.

> A spring was sticking out of the faded sofa cushion, coiled.

Coiled is too far away from the word it's modifying, *spring*. To make this sentence easier to understand, the misplaced modifier should be moved closer to the word it's describing.

>   coiled
> A ˄spring was sticking out of the faded sofa cushion, ~~coiled~~.

Modifying phrases or clauses can also be misplaced.

> Daniel saw a strange-looking bird using his new binoculars.

The modifying phrase "using his new binoculars" is supposed to be describing Daniel, but it is misplaced in the sentence. As a result, the meaning of the sentence completely changes to suggest that a bird was using Daniel's new binoculars.

To fix the misplaced modifier, move it as close as possible to *Daniel* so that the sentence makes sense.

> Using his new binoculars,
> ˄Daniel saw a strange-looking bird ~~using his new binoculars.~~

Sometimes, a misplaced modifier is hard to spot because the meaning of the sentence could still be logical.

> The books in the library cannot be purchased.

> The books cannot be purchased in the library.

Both of these sentences make sense. The first sentence implies that none of the books in the library can be bought. The second sentence implies that books can be purchased, just not in the library. You should carefully read your sentences and look for misplaced modifiers to make sure you're expressing your thoughts clearly.

Exercise

Practice revising the sentences below so that the modifier is not misplaced. Underline the modifier and draw an arrow to the correct placement in the sentence.

There are hundreds of signatures from local business owners on the county website's petition.

The gray tabby cat stared at me as I got in my car, sitting in the window.

He tried to delete the awkward voicemail he had just left, desperately.

Dangling Modifiers

A dangling modifier happens when the word being modified is missing from the sentence.

> After reading through the budget, the miscalculation was discovered.

The modifier in this sentence is "After reading through the budget," but it's dangling because it has nothing to modify. *Who is reading through the budget?*

To correct a dangling modifier, add the missing information as close to the modifier as possible.

> *the accountant discovered the miscalculation*
> After reading through the budget, ~~the miscalculation~~
>
> ~~was discovered.~~

Sometimes, the best way to fix a dangling modifier is to add the missing information to the modifier itself.

> Since opening the new restaurant, the menu has changed every year.

The menu didn't open the restaurant, so who did?

the Myers opened
Since ~~opening~~ the new restaurant, the menu has changed

every year.

Here are a few more examples:

Dangling Modifier:	Looking at her watch constantly, the minute hand seemed to be frozen.
Revised:	Looking at her watch constantly, Jan thought the minute hand seemed to be frozen.
Dangling Modifier:	By training diligently, chances of reaching the championship have increased.
Revised:	By training diligently, the team's chances of reaching the championship have increased.

Chapter 9

Word Choice

9a Clarity and Conciseness

While academic and professional documents may be formal, they should not be confusing. You don't need to use complicated language to sound "smarter." Carefully choosing your words to create clear and concise sentences will improve your writing more effectively than using flowery or over-complicated language.

Clear Words

When writing is "clear," it's easy to understand because the meaning is obvious. Take a look at these sentences:

> This stratagem will advocate tandem techniques to diminish building perpetuation expenditures.

> This proposal will suggest two ways to reduce building maintenance cost.

The second sentence is clear, or easy to understand. In contrast, the first sentence is confusing; the meaning is not obvious. This is because it uses words like *tandem* and *expenditures* when simpler words like *two* and *costs* would work just as well.

Exercise

Read the following pairs of sentences and circle the one that uses clear words.

Remember to return the lab equipment to the cabinet at the end of class.

Remember to reinstate the laboratory accouterments in the repository at the termination of class.

My cellular device commenced pealing in the midsection of the allocution.

My phone started ringing in the middle of the lecture.

Jargon

"Jargon" is overly technical language, and using it can make writing unclear. Here's an example:

> The nomenclature of the *Acer rubrum* is derived from the visual perceptual property of the principal lateral appendages of its stems during the temperate season of autumn.

Can you tell what this sentence says? It's explaining that red maples get their name from their leaves, which turn red in the fall. However, figuring this out is difficult because of scientific jargon like *"Acer rubrum"* and "principal lateral appendages." Unless the author is writing to an audience of other scientists, this language is unnecessary.

Conciseness

To be "concise" means to communicate as much information as possible with the least amount of words. The opposite of concise is wordy. Wordy writing uses more words and phrases than necessary. Take a look at this paragraph:

> I wanted to see if you would be willing to meet with me for just a couple minutes tomorrow in the afternoon at 2:15 or sometime around then. I would really appreciate being able to hear what you think about the progress I've made with the first draft of the paper that I've been writing. Due to the fact that I am having some trouble with organizing my paragraphs, I am hoping that you can help me. It would be great if I could come to your office after class tomorrow afternoon, but I can also meet at another time if it would work better for you.

The author circles around the meaning of each sentence, using four or five words when just one is required. Here are some examples of especially wordy phrases:

> just a couple minutes tomorrow in the afternoon at 2:15 or sometime around then

> the first draft of the paper that I've been writing

Due to the fact that I am having some trouble with organizing my paragraphs

Here is a more concise version of the same paragraph:

Are you available for a brief meeting around 2:15 tomorrow afternoon? I would like to hear your feedback on my first draft of Essay #3. I am having trouble organizing my paragraphs and would appreciate your help. If another time would be better, please let me know.

A concise sentence is not always short; you don't want to leave out important information. Instead, focus on using words that state exactly what you want to say.

Here's another example of a paragraph that has been changed from wordy to concise:

Last July, ~~in the summer,~~ I visited my friend, ~~whose first name is~~ Ben. At the time, he was living in New York and interning as a writer at *The Powder Magazine*, ~~which is a magazine~~. We did typical tourist activities ~~such as going to see~~ *like visiting* the Statue of Liberty and Times Square. The whole time, I felt like I was on ~~the set of a movie~~ *a movie set*.

Take a look at this table of common wordy phrases and the concise version

Wordy	Concise
the professors who teach at Harvard Law School	professors at Harvard Law School
owing to the fact that	because
the type of information used for test purposes	used for tests
Elizabeth Cady Stanton was a woman who wrote	Elizabeth Cady Stanton wrote
a movie that is exciting	an exciting movie

Wordy	Concise
situations that could be considered exceptions	exceptions
worked as a manager	managed

Unnecessary Repetition

The common term for unnecessary repetition is "redundancy." This concept often overlaps with conciseness and wordiness. Take a look at this example:

> It's a true fact that narwhals only have two teeth.

True and *fact* mean essentially the same thing, so the phrase "true fact" is redundant. To correct this, remove either word.

> It's a fact that narwhals only have two teeth.

> It's true that narwhals only have two teeth.

Redundancy can happen within a few words, like using *true* and *fact* together. It can also happen within a phrase or an entire paragraph if an idea or explanation is written more than once. Identifying and removing redundancy will make your writing clear and concise.

Here are some common redundant phrases:

Redundant	Revised
12 o'clock midnight/noon	midnight/noon
advance warning	warning
complete opposite	opposite
past history	history
unexpected surprise	surprise
same exact	exact
free gift	gift
ask a question	ask
consensus of opinion	consensus
end result	result
plan ahead	plan

Redundant	Revised
revert back	revert
HIV virus	HIV (Human Immunodeficiency Virus)
PIN number	PIN (Personal Identification Number)

9b Vague vs. Vivid Words

When something is "vague," it is unconfirmed or unclear. In writing, vague words are unclear because they are too general. In contrast, vivid words are specific and interesting. "Vivid" means colorful or bright.

In writing, it's important to use language that is both interesting and accurate. Choosing words that are vivid, not vague, will improve your sentences in two ways. First, it will capture the attention of your audience. Second, it will help you effectively communicate your ideas.

Vague vs. Vivid Nouns

Choosing specific nouns will make your writing more vivid. Take a look at these examples:

Vague Nouns	Vivid Nouns
guy	best friend
organization	European Union
stuff	clutter
pet	iguana
show	*Pushing Daisies*
people	mechanics

Vague vs. Vivid Verbs

Using specific action verbs will also make your writing more vivid. Take a look at these example

Vague Verbs	Vivid Verbs
was walking	was striding
sat	slumped
say	argue
found	discovered
am going	am traveling
went	sprinted

Vague vs. Vivid Adjectives and Adverbs

Another way to write vividly is to use unique adjectives and adverbs. Words like *nice* and *good* are often overused.

Vague	Vivid
nice	thoughtful
very	extremely
dark	pitch black
cold	frigid
really	undoubtedly
some	twenty-five

Exercise

Try using vivid nouns, verbs, adjectives, and adverbs to re-write the following sentences:

The bear got the fish in the water.

A girl talked quickly about her fun weekend.

My roommate said he is sad because our team lost the game.

9c Choosing Correct Words

To make sure you effectively communicate your ideas, it's important to use the most appropriate words. Try downloading a trustworthy dictionary app on your phone, bookmarking a reference website on your browser, or carrying a pocket-sized reference with you. This will help you choose the best word while you're writing.

Tone

Tone is a positive, negative, or neutral attitude. Just like you use your voice to communicate a certain tone when speaking, you can use words to do the same thing when writing.

> The new skyscraper was impressive.

> The new skyscraper was overwhelming.

In these sentences, one word changes the tone of the whole sentence. *Impressive* has a positive tone, but *overwhelming* has a negative tone.

It's a common mistake to use a word that has the wrong tone, but this can confuse your reader and even yourself.

> Jeremy leered out the window to see if the mail truck had come.

The word *leered* almost always has a negative tone, which means it doesn't fit with a neutral activity like looking for the mail truck. There's another word with a more appropriate tone.

> *glanced*
> Jeremy ~~leered~~ out the window to see if the mail truck
>
> had come.

Sometimes, a word doesn't have a *wrong* tone; there's just another word that would fit even better.

> My two-year-old son is always running around, but today he was ready for his afternoon respite.

> My two-year-old son is always running around, but today he was ready for his afternoon nap.

These sentences use *respite* and *nap*, which both have a neutral or even positive tone. However, *respite* is too formal in this context. *Nap* is a better word because it fits the context and the casual tone of the rest of the sentence.

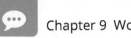

Exercise

Label the following words as *positive, negative,* or *neutral.* Use a dictionary and/or thesaurus for some extra guidance.

enthusiastic

gloomy

walk

mimic

sneer

Clichés

A cliché is something that has been used so much that it is no longer original or interesting. Think of a song you used to like but are tired of now. You probably don't like the song anymore because you heard it over and over. A cliché works the same way.

A cliché can be an event or even an idea, like the cliché of two people disliking each other and then eventually falling in love; this is common in movies, TV shows, and books. However, many clichés are phrases.

The car raced around the track at the speed of light.

There may be times when using a cliché is appropriate. For example, an author might intentionally use clichés to make a point. Reinventing a cliché can also be an effective writing strategy.

My sister was frightened to death by the haunted house, but I was frightened to life; I sprinted through the dark hallways and out the door.

In this sentence, the writer reinvents the cliché "frightened to death" by changing it to "frightened to life," which adds more interest to the sentence.

Most of the time, though, writing that uses clichés comes across as predictable or boring.

Because they're so prevalent, most clichés are easy to spot. If you catch yourself using a cliché, delete it completely or replace it with a more original phrase. Here are a few more examples of clichés:

Throughout history

In the nick of time

The time of my life

Opposites attract

Raining cats and dogs

Cool as a cucumber

Light as a feather

Actions speak louder than words

Love is blind

Think outside the box

The early bird catches the worm

Old habits die hard

A picture is worth a thousand words

Beauty is in the eye of the beholder

9d Inclusive Language

Inclusive language is respectful of people's differences. The opposite of **inclusive** language is **exclusive** language. Exclusive language disrespectfully refers to a person's gender, ethnicity or culture, physical or mental ability, or sexual orientation.

If a text uses exclusive language, it might be a sign of bias. However, writing that uses inclusive language will come across as more trustworthy and balanced.

Gender

Terms

A gender-specific word like *mankind* is a type of exclusive language because it refers specifically to men and excludes women.

Additionally, exclusive language uses separate terms to describe men and women, even though the words have the same meaning. For example, *shepherd* refers to a male shepherd, and *shepherdess* refers to a female shepherd, even though the job is the same.

Inclusive language uses gender-neutral terms to describe men and women, such as *humankind*. "Gender-neutral" means that it does not refer specifically to men or to women.

Gender-Specific	Gender-Neutral
actor, actress	actor
doctor, lady doctor	doctor
male nurse, nurse	nurse
policeman, policewoman	police officer
waiter, waitress	waiter

Pronouns

If a text is clearly referring to men or women, use the appropriate pronoun. However, exclusive language uses a male personal pronoun as the default if someone's gender is unknown.

Exclusive: If a person needs to make a phone call, he can step outside.

Inclusive language uses a gender-neutral pronoun when a person's gender is unknown. There are two options for using inclusive pronouns.

Use the term *he or she*.

When a person needs to make a phone call, he or she can step outside.

Make the subject plural and use a gender-neutral pronoun.

When people need to make a phone call, they can step outside.

Some people do not self-identify as male or female. In that case, you should find out which pronoun they prefer.

Stereotypes

Inclusive language does not use stereotypes based on gender. A stereotype is an over-simplified idea about a group of people. Because each person is a unique individual, general statements about a group of people are often inaccurate and disrespectful.

Exclusive: The high number of accidents involving female drivers this year gives credibility to the saying that women can't drive.

Exclusive: Brian is a real man; he loves hunting, fishing, and camping.

These sentence clearly use stereotypes about both men and women. The first sentence uses a stereotype about all women being bad drivers. The second sentence uses a stereotype about all men enjoying certain activities.

Unrelated Information

Writing that refers to a person's gender, when this information is unnecessary, is using exclusive language.

Exclusive: The accident was caused when the driver, a woman, veered into the other lane.

This sentence refers to the driver's gender, even though this information is unnecessary for the meaning of the sentence.

Inclusive language only mentions someone's gender when it is essential to the meaning of the text.

Ethnicity or Culture

Terms

One way to use exclusive language about ethnicity or culture is using outdated, inaccurate, or insulting terms. For example, during the First and Second World Wars, it became popular among many Americans to call Germans *Krauts*, a derogatory label derived from *sauerkraut*. Here is a more modern example:

Exclusive: *Atanarjuat* is a widely-acclaimed film based
            Inuit
            on an ~~Eskimo~~ legend passed down from

            generation to generation.

Eskimo is an outdated term that incorrectly groups together several distinct indigenous people groups. *Inuit* is a more accurate term.

Inclusive language uses the correct term to refer to someone's ethnicity. If you are unsure which term to use, look up the information from a reputable source. Usually, people of that ethnicity or culture can tell you which term they prefer.

Stereotypes

Exclusive language makes assumptions about people based on their ethnicity or culture. For example, using a stereotype about a person with a certain ethnic background is inappropriate.

Exclusive: Ryan is Asian, so he's probably going to get an *A* on the math exam.

Whether a stereotype seems negative or positive, it's disrespectful to make assumptions about someone based on his or her ethnicity.

Unrelated Information

Exclusive language about ethnicity or culture can be subtle. For example, referring to someone's ethnicity in an unrelated comment is an example of exclusive language.

Exclusive: Yesterday, police arrested Greg Lopez, a Colombian man who lives in Lebanon, PA, on armed robbery charges.

In this sentence, the suspect's ethnicity has nothing to do with his crime.

Inclusive language refers to someone's ethnicity or culture only when it is essential to the meaning of the text.

Inclusive: Chef Candice Aquino says that her cooking is inspired by her heritage because both of her parents were born in the Philippines.

Physical or Mental Ability

Exclusive language equates people with their physical or mental ability.

Exclusive: Percy Jackson is a dyslexic.

This statement disrespectfully refers to Percy's physical or mental ability by equating him with his condition: "a dyslexic."

Inclusive language puts the person first instead of defining them by their disability. Information about someone's physical or mental ability should only be included when it's relevant to the purpose of the sentence.

Using medical terms inaccurately is also an example of exclusive language.

Exclusive: She still isn't satisfied with the layout; she's so OCD.

Exclusive: The traffic light was clearly red; is he blind?

Unless the people in these sentences have been officially diagnosed, this is exclusive language. Even if these people do have a medical condition, mentioning it in a disrespectful or insulting way would still be a type of exclusive language.

One way to use inclusive language is to use a term like "accessible parking spots" instead of "disabled parking spots." This emphasizes the accessibility of the parking spot, not the limitations of the person.

Sexual Orientation

Inclusive language does not mention someone's sexual orientation when this information is irrelevant.

Exclusive: My cousin, who's gay, is graduating this spring.

Inclusive: My cousin is graduating this spring.

This sentence uses exclusive language because the sexual orientation of the cousin is completely unnecessary to the meaning of the sentence.

Inclusive language also uses respectful terms.

Exclusive	Inclusive
gay couple	couple
his husband/her wife	spouse, partner

If you need to discuss sexual orientation, use a resource like the GLAAD organization to research inclusive terms.

9e Commonly Misused Words

These words are commonly misused because their meanings are closely related.

Between and Among

Between is a preposition that shows a relationship between two people or things.

Markham requested that all communication between the defendants should be approved by him first.

The hammock was tied between two large trees.

Among is a preposition that shows relationships between more than two people or things.

I divided the Halloween candy equally among my three children.

Competition was fierce among the runners.

Borrow and Lend

Borrow is a verb that means "to take temporarily."

After borrowing millions of dollars from the European Union, Greek banks began to fail.

My little brother always wants to borrow my stuff.

Lend is a verb that means "to give temporarily."

Could you lend me your truck when I move?

The bank agreed to lend her money to open a restaurant.

Come and Go

Come is a noun that indicates movement toward the speaker.

Are you planning to come to my house after work?

The wary zebra watched the lioness come closer to the herd.

Go is a verb that indicates movement away from the speaker.

Don't go while it's still snowing outside.

Cary couldn't wait to go to Disney World.

Fewer and Less

Fewer compares items that can be counted.

There are three fewer volunteers than last time.

There are fewer pandas in the wild than there were twenty years ago.

Less compares items that cannot be counted.

This year, people have been donating less than usual.

There is less crime in the city since the new mayor was elected.

Lie and Lay

Lie is a noun that means "to recline."

> The nurse asked the patient to lie still during the MRI.

> After the large meal, we decided to lie down for a nap.

Lay is a noun that means "to set down."

> You can lay your coats on the bed.

> Lay the cement on the south side of the building.

Chapter 10

Shifts in Tense and Person

10a Consistency in Tense

Verb Tense

Verb tenses indicate when an action took place: past, present, or future. Another way to think of tense is as an indication of *time*.

Past	Present	Future
hated	hate	will hate
ran	run	will run
took	take	will take

Here's how verb tenses look in a sentence:

Past	Salman called the office.
Present	Salman calls the office.
Future	Salman will call the office.

Purposes of Tense

Tense	Type of Writing
Present	Narrative or story Literary analysis or discussion
Past	Event report Reflection on past experience
Future	Plans Instructions

Present

Present tense is often used in narratives or stories because it makes readers feel as if the events are taking place right before their eyes. Think of present tense in writing as the equivalent of a live video feed.

> Kit approaches the closed door. He looks with wide eyes at the paint peeling off the frame and the long scratches gouged in the boards beneath his feet. Tentatively, he lifts his hand and takes a deep breath. His fist hovers uncertainly in the air. Suddenly, he raps his knuckles loudly on the warped wood. His heart races as he hears heavy footsteps on the other side of the door.

The present tense is also used for analyzing literature. The events of the book, and any author analysis, should be discussed using the present tense.

> F. Scott Fitzgerald's exploration of the American Dream is evident when Jay Gatsby speaks about Daisy Buchanan. Gatsby's idealized version of Daisy is the motivation for— and the fulfillment of—all of his ambitions.

Past

The past tense is used to report an event or reflect on a past experience.

> Since 73% of registered voters participated in last night's election, voter turnout was at an all-time high.

> My father always told the story about the time he camped in the Blue Ridge Mountains with his brothers and saw a bear.

Many works of fiction are also written in the past tense.

Future

Future tense is used to describe anything that has not yet happened, like plans or instructions.

> During our next meeting, we will discuss decorating ideas for the upcoming show.

Part A will connect to Part B to form the base of the bookshelf.

Exercise

Rewrite the sentences below so that they all use the past tense.

My new puppy will chew on the chair legs.

He drops his phone on the pavement two days after buying it.

The Ferris wheel spins slowly in the humid summer night.

Inconsistent Tense

Switching tenses in the middle of a thought is awkward.

> I felt my heart racing as Devonte approached my desk on the first day of the semester. My best friend snickered because she knew how much I liked him. Suddenly, he grabs the seat to my right and sits down.

In this paragraph, the action is happening in the past, but the last sentence uses the present tense. This interrupts the flow of the writing.

Switching tenses can also happen within a sentence.

Inconsistent Tense	As I walk down the hall to refill my water bottle, I tripped and fell in front of the open door of a classroom.

Consistent Tense	As I walked down the hall to refill my water bottle, I tripped and fell in front of the open door of a classroom.
Consistent Tense	As I walk down the hall to refill my water bottle, I trip and fall in front of the open door of a classroom.

In order to communicate your main idea effectively, make sure you use consistent tense.

Appropriate Tense Shifts

Sometimes, shifting tenses within a sentence or paragraph is necessary.

To describe events that happened at two different points in time, it's appropriate to use different verb tense.

> We took inventory of the women's department last week, and we are working through the men's department now.

To show that a current or future action is the result of a past action, shifting tenses is also appropriate.

> Josh left the towels out in the rain last night, so Karen is drying them at the laundromat now.

> I just realized that the cupcakes taste strange because they are missing some ingredients. Next time, I will pay closer attention to the recipe.

10b Consistency in Person

Personal Pronouns

Personal pronouns can be first-person, second-person, or third-person. Another way to think of person is as *perspective*. A text can be written from *my* perspective (first-person), *your* perspective (second-person), or *their* perspective (third-person).

Number	First Person	Second Person	Third Person
Singular	I, me, my, mine	you, your, yours	he, him, his
Plural	we, us, our, ours	you, your, yours	she, her, hers
			it, its
			they, them, their, theirs

All nouns are considered third-person.

Here's what personal pronouns look like in a sentence:

First person	We had a waffle bar at our wedding reception.
Second person	You had a waffle bar at your wedding reception.
Third person	They had a waffle bar at their wedding reception.

Purposes of Person

Different perspectives are appropriate for different types of writing. In general, certain types of writing are commonly written in a particular person:

Perspective	Writing Type
First-person	Informal writing
	Personal reflection
Second-person	Instructions
	Advice
Third-person	Formal academic writing
	Business writing

Inconsistent Person

If the perspective of a text shifts frequently, it can be hard to follow.

> After the graduates received their degrees, 80% of us moved to new cities.

> I will never forget my first trip to Disney World. I was so excited to try out all of the rides. You could get a pass for access to different rides in multiple parks.

In the first example, *graduates* is third-person because all nouns are third-person, and *their* is a third-person pronoun. However, *us* is a first-person pronoun. **Antecedents** are the words that pronouns replace; since *graduates* is the antecedent, the personal pronouns in this sentence that are replacing *graduate* need to be consistently third-person.

In the second example, the last sentence switches from using first-person pronouns *I* and *my* to second-person pronoun *you*.

> After the graduates received their degrees, 80% of ~~us~~ *them*
>
> moved to new cities.

> I will never forget my first trip to Disney World. I was so
>
> excited to try out all of the rides. ~~You~~ *I* could get a pass for
>
> access to different rides in multiple parks.

Exercise

Rewrite the sentences below so that they all use *plural, first-person* pronouns.

She always walks to the store because her house is only two blocks away.

They are opening a restaurant in their neighborhood.

Tell me how much the tickets cost so I can write it down.

121

Grammar Basics

Chapter 11

Parts of Speech

11a Nouns

A noun is a word that represents a person, place, thing, or idea.
Nouns are the *who* and *what* in a sentence. There are four main
categories of nouns:

- Common and proper nouns
- Singular and plural nouns
- Count and non-count nouns
- Compound nouns

There are also three basic ways to use nouns in a sentence:

- Nouns as subjects
- Nouns as objects
- Nouns as adjectives

Common and Proper Nouns

Common nouns refer to non-specific people, places, things,
or ideas. Because these nouns are general, they do not start
with a capital letter unless they are located at the beginning of
a sentence.

> Visitors to the aquarium love to watch the playful otters.

> Otters are playful animals; people love to watch them.

Proper nouns refer to specific people, places, things, or ideas.
These nouns always start with a capital letter.

> The newest addition to the aquarium is an otter
> named Theo.

> Theo was found abandoned just a few miles from
> the aquarium.

Take a look at these examples of common and proper nouns.

Common Nouns	Proper Nouns
author	J.K. Rowling
activist	Martin Luther King, Jr.
friend	Chandler
state	Tennessee
movie	*Interstellar*
city	St. Louis
website	*Reddit*
dog	Clifford

Singular and Plural Nouns

Singular nouns refer to one (single) person, place, thing, or idea.

The delicious cake had three layers.

Next week, the mayor is going to make an announcement.

Plural nouns refer to multiple people, places, things, or ideas.

All of the presidential candidates participated in the debate.

Seagulls swarmed the unsuspecting tourists.

Take a look at these examples of singular and plural nouns.

Singular Nouns	Plural Nouns
David Bowie	musicians
leader	leaders
tablet	tablets
Mt. Rushmore	monuments
flock	flocks
Taco Bell	restaurants
shoe	shoes
Canadian	Canadians

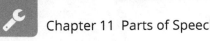

Count and Non-Count Nouns

Like the name indicates, count nouns are nouns that can be counted. Non-count nouns are nouns that cannot be counted. Here are some examples:

Count Nouns	Non-count Nouns
arrow	gravity
update	milk
pie	soccer
singer	honesty
game	electricity

To test whether a noun is count or non-count, add a number in front. For example, it makes sense to say "three updates," but not "three gravities."

Exercise

Add numbers in front of the following nouns to determine if they are count or non-count.

_____   valley

_____   mud

_____   wish

_____   atmosphere

Compound Nouns

Compound nouns are nouns that are made up of more than one word. Some compound nouns are joined together into one word. Consider these examples:

sunrise   bedroom

softball   mailbox

Other compound nouns are separated by spaces or hyphens:

bus stop   lamp post

sister-in-law   dry-cleaner

Nouns as Subjects

A noun can act as the subject of a sentence. A subject is *whom* or *what* a sentence is about.

The shortest road leads to home.

Adam is throwing a party on the 4th of July.

The booth in the corner is reserved.

Three concerts are scheduled for this month.

Nouns as Objects

Nouns can act as objects: direct objects and objects of prepositions. A direct object receives the action of a verb.

I locked the door behind me.

In this sentence, *door* is a noun acting as a direct object because it is receiving the action of being locked. Take a look at a few more examples:

Gray clouds filled the sky.

The goalie intently watched the kicker.

An object of a preposition completes the meaning of a prepositional phrase.

The suitcases were displayed in the window.

In this sentence, *window* is a noun acting as an object of the preposition because it completes the meaning of the prepositional phrase "in the window." Take a look at a few more examples:

The bicyclist sped down the road.

On the weekend, I love watching movies in my pajamas.

Nouns as Adjectives

Nouns can act as adjectives by describing other nouns or pronouns.

> This Christmas, I bought a phone case for my dad.

In this sentence, *phone* is a noun acting as an adjective because it is describing another noun: *case*. Take a look at a few more examples:

> Two restaurants and one gas station have opened this month.

> The basketball game went into triple overtime.

11b Pronouns

A pronoun is a word that takes the place of a noun in a sentence. Another word for this replaced noun is "antecedent."

> Vera said that Vera wants to visit the Rocky Mountains.

> Vera said that she wants to visit the Rocky Mountains.

In this sentence, *Vera* is the antecedent being replaced by the pronoun *she*.

Just like nouns, pronouns can represent people, places, things, or ideas. There are three primary types of pronouns:

- Personal pronouns
- Relative pronouns
- Indefinite pronouns

Personal Pronouns

Personal pronouns are called personal because they rename a specific person, animal, object, or place.

> After the interview, I began transcribing the audio recording into a text document.

> Did you see the accident on the highway?

Personal pronouns change form depending on how they are used in a sentence. To know which form to use, consider the four ways that pronouns can be categorized:

- Number
- Person
- Gender
- Case

Number

When pronouns are divided by number, they are separated into two groups: singular and plural. Singular pronouns refer to one (single) person or object. Plural pronouns refer to multiple people or objects.

Singular	Plural
I, me, my, mine	we, us, our, ours
you, your, yours	you, your, yours
he, him, his	they, them, their, theirs
she, her, hers	
it, its	

Singular	The guest speaker glanced at his notes.
Plural	The dancers knew they needed to practice the routine again.

Person

When pronouns are divided by person, they are separated into three groups: first-, second-, and third-person. Use first-person pronouns to talk about yourself, second-person pronouns when talking directly to someone else, and third-person pronouns for everyone else.

First-Person	Second-Person	Third-Person
I, me, my, mine	you, your, yours	he, him, his
we, us, our, ours		she, her, hers
		it, its
		they, them, their, theirs

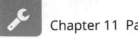

First-person	The single from our next album will be released next week.
Second-person	Remember to keep track of all your account passwords.
Third-person	She is trying out for the tennis team.

Gender

When pronouns are divided by gender, they are separated into three groups: male, female, and neutral. Only third-person pronouns have gender.

Male	Female	Neutral
he, him, his	she, her, hers	I, me, my, mine
		we, us, our, ours
		you, your, yours
		it, its
		they, them, their, theirs

Male	The toddler asked his mother for a cookie.
Female	Harper said that one day she planned to design a roller coaster.
Neutral	In the third movie, the armies have gathered for their final battle.

Case

When pronouns are divided by case, they are separated into three groups: subjective, objective, and possessive.

Subjective	Objective	Possessive
I, we	me, us	my, mine
you	you	your, yours
he, she, it	him, her, it	his, her, hers, its
they	them	their, theirs

Subjective pronouns act as the subject of a sentence.

> We bought ice cream and cookies at the store.

> Tomorrow, she is having surgery.

Objective case pronouns act as objects of a preposition or verb.

> The instructor gave us a study guide.

> Send the new textbooks to them.

Possessive case pronouns act as possessive adjectives.

> I left my laundry in the dryer.

> The director promoted his new movie.

Indefinite Pronouns

Indefinite pronouns don't rename a specific noun, and they are divided into three groups: singular, plural, and both.

Singular		Plural	Both
anybody	nobody	both	all
anyone	no one	few	any
anything	nothing	many	most
each	somebody	several	none
everybody	someone		some
everyone	something		
everything			

Singular	Everyone is required to attend the assembly on Monday morning.
Plural	Several volunteered to address the envelopes.
Both	Kylie was interested in signing up for most of the special offers.
Both	The rug covered most of the cold floor.

Relative Pronouns

Relative pronouns introduce dependent clauses, which are groups of words that do not express a complete thought. There are seven relative pronouns:

that	whoever
which	whom
whichever	whomever
who	

Take a look at this example:

> During the archaeological dig on Easter Island, the team found two tablets that were covered in an ancient language called Rongorongo.

In this sentence, *that* is a relative pronoun introducing the dependent clause "were covered in an ancient language called Rongorongo."

Who and *whom* are the only relative pronouns that have a specific case. *Who* is a subjective case pronoun, and *whom* is an objective case pronoun. If you're not sure which one to use, determine how the pronoun is being used inside the sentence; is it an object of a preposition or verb, or is it the subject? You can also try substituting *he* or *she* for *who* and *him* or *her* for *whom*.

> Who is directing this movie?

> She is directing this movie.

> You are meeting whom at the park?

> You are meeting him at the park.

11c Verbs

Verbs are words that represent actions, relationships, or states of being. There are three main types of verbs:

- Action verbs
- Helping verbs
- Linking verbs

Action Verbs

Action verbs show physical or mental action.

> After the race, Jordan guzzled a liter of water.

> My friend drives a twelve-year-old car.

> During the final exam, most of the students struggled with the essay question.

Some action verbs have direct objects.

> Harmony accidentally threw the Frisbee over the fence.

Frisbee **is the direct object because it is receiving the action of the verb:** *threw*. **Here are a few more examples of action verbs with direct objects.**

> The dog's wagging tail knocked the cup off the coffee table.

> The quarterback launched the ball towards the running back.

Some verbs that have direct objects will also have indirect objects.

> The audience gave Chef Franke a standing ovation after the demonstration.

Chef Franke **is the indirect object because he is receiving the direct object:** *ovation*. **Here are a few more examples with indirect objects.**

> Kendra passed her sister the sunglasses.

> Critics awarded the movie five stars.

Note that action verbs, direct objects, and indirect objects will never appear inside a prepositional phrase.

> (On Mother's Day), the children brought their mother breakfast (in bed).

In this sentence, the prepositional phrases are surrounded by parentheses. *Brought* is the action verb, *breakfast* is the direct object, and *mother* is the indirect object.

Linking Verbs

Linking verbs link a subject to its description.

> My best friend is a talented musician.

> The guests are waiting for invitations.

> In the morning, the city is foggy and gray.

Many linking verbs are forms of the word *be*:

am	are	were
is	was	

Some verbs can function either as linking or action verbs.

Action Verb	The hikers smelled the campfire from over two miles away.
Linking Verb	The hikers smelled terrible after their two-day trip.

In the first sentence, the hikers are actually using their noses to smell something, so *smelled* is an action verb. In the second sentence, the description *terrible* is being linked to the hikers, so *smelled* is a linking verb.

Here is a list of words that commonly function as both action and linking verbs:

appear	look	sound
become	remain	stay
feel	seem	taste
grow	smell	

Helping Verbs

Some verbs are made up of more than two words. In these cases, one of those words is probably a helping verb. Helping verbs change the form of a main verb so that it makes grammatical sense for that sentence.

Without Helping Verb The group of volunteers sorted the box of donations.

With Helping Verb The group of volunteers were sorting the box of donations.

Here is a list of common helping verbs:

am	do	must
are	does	shall
be	had	should
been	has	was
being	have	were
can	is	will
could	may	would
did	might	

Some verbs can function either as helping or linking verbs.

In the first sentence, the verb *was* is helping the main verb *mowing*. In the second sentence, the verb *was* is linking the description *tired* to the subject.

11d Adjectives

Identifying Adjectives

Adjectives are words that describe nouns or pronouns. They answer the following questions:

- Which one?
- What kind?
- How many/much?
- Whose?

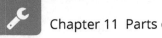

Use these questions to determine whether or not a word is an adjective.

Ben checked the car tires for punctures.

In this sentence, *car* is an adjective because it answers the question "what kind of tires?" Here's another example:

The restaurant had been open for eighty years.

In this sentence, *eighty* is an adjective because it answers the question "how many years?"

Usually, adjectives appear right before or after the word they describe. However, adjectives can also appear later in a sentence, after a linking verb.

Several people were fidgety at work.

In this sentence, *fidgety* is an adjective connected to *people* by the linking verb *were*.

Articles

Articles are a special type of adjective. The following words are articles:

a   an   the

Narcolepsy is a disease that can cause sleep paralysis.

The plumber realized that the pipe fittings were the wrong size.

Comparisons

When adjectives are used to compare two or more items, the form of the adjective changes.

This sandwich is delicious.

This sandwich is more delicious than the one I ate yesterday.

This sandwich is the most delicious one I've ever eaten.

Two Items	More Than Two Items
more	most
–er	–est

When you are comparing two items, add the suffix –er to the end of the word. For some adjectives, like *talented*, adding –er would not be correct. If so, add the word *more* before the adjective instead.

> The survey found that this year's customers are happier than
> last year's.

> This song is more upbeat than the first one.

When you are comparing more than two items, add the suffix –est to the end of the word. For some adjectives, like *foreboding*, adding –est would not be correct. If so, add the word *most* before the adjective instead.

> Out of the top three cross-country runners, Hernando is the fastest.

> My aunt is the most enthusiastic hockey fan in our family.

Comparisons using *good* and *bad* are formed in a slightly different way.

Good	good	→	better	→	best
Bad	bad	→	worse	→	worst

11e Adverbs

Identifying Adverbs

Adverbs are words that describe verbs, adjectives, or other adverbs. They answer the following questions:

- When?
- Where?
- Why?

- How?
- How often?

Use these questions to determine whether or not a word is an adverb.

> The nurse walked slowly down the hallway.

In this sentence, *slowly* is an adverb because it answers the question "how did the nurse walk?" Here's another example:

> With a shout, the tennis player angrily threw down her racket.

In this sentence, *angrily* is an adverb because it answers the question "how did the tennis player throw down her racket?"

Not all adverbs end in *–ly*. Take a look at this example:

> I went to the grocery story yesterday.

In this sentence, *yesterday* is an adverb because it answers the question "when did I go to the store?" Take a look at a few more examples of adverbs that do not end in *–ly*.

> The groundhog looked down and saw its own shadow.

> You can put your assignment here.

Besides verbs, adverbs also describe adjectives and adverbs.

> The new book by Paisley Framer looks really interesting.

In this sentence, *really* is an adverb describing the adjective *interesting*. Take a look at a few more examples:

Describing Adjectives	The new engine is more powerful than last year's.
	My kids think this is a really funny cartoon.
Describing Adverbs	My niece can sing very well.
	The radio host spoke unusually quickly.

Negative Words

The following negative words are adverbs.

never   not

These words sometimes appear in the middle of a verb.

The choir had never performed in front of so many people.

Once a house is 75% done, the builder will not make any changes to the floorplan.

Comparisons

When adverbs are used to compare two or more items, the form of the adverb changes.

Two Items	More Than Two Items
more	most
-er	-est

When you are comparing two items, add the suffix *–er* to the end of the word. For adverbs that end in *–ly*, adding *–er* would not be correct. If so, add the word *more* before the adverb instead.

The new driver drove more carefully than he had yesterday.

To make the varsity swim team, she had to train harder than last year.

When you are comparing more than two items, add the suffix *–est* to the end of the word. For adverbs that end in *–ly*, adding *–est* would not be correct. If so, add the word *most* before the adverb instead.

Of all the store employees, the café staff worked the most diligently.

Out of all the people at the holiday party, the Coopers stayed the longest.

Comparisons using *well* and *badly* are formed in a slightly different way.

Well	well	→	better	→	best
Badly	badly	→	worse	→	worst

11f Prepositions

Common Prepositions

Prepositions are words that show relationships among people, places, things, and ideas. Here is a list of common prepositions:

about	but	outside
above	by	over
across	down	past
after	during	since
against	except	through
along	for	throughout
among	from	to
around	in	toward
at	inside	under
before	into	underneath
behind	like	until
below	near	up
beneath	off	upon
beside	of	with
between	on	within
beyond	onto	without

Sometimes, the relationships that prepositions show are physical locations.

The research team met in Harvard's genetic laboratory.

I accidentally left my phone on my bed.

Marcy and Yumi met their friends outside the theater.

However, prepositions also show relationships such as time.

The search party began sweeping the area at noon.

Twelve years have passed since the team's last Final Four appearance.

The party will begin after the fireworks show.

Basic Prepositional Phrases

A prepositional phrase is a group of related words that begins with a preposition and ends with a noun or pronoun. The noun or pronoun that ends a prepositional phrase is called the object of the preposition.

The crowd on the train platform was growing.

This sentence has one prepositional phrase: "on the train platform." *On* is the preposition, and *platform* is a noun acting as the object of the preposition. *The* is an article, and *train* is a noun acting as an adjective; both are describing *platform*. Here are a few more examples:

I found a mysterious package on my doorstep after work.

Kiely Robinson is the author of two best-selling novels about her experiences in Peru.

Remember, the subject and verb of a sentence will never appear inside a prepositional phrase.

Prepositional Phrases as Adjectives

In a sentence, prepositional phrases can function as adjectives. Just like regular adjectives, these prepositional phrases will describe a noun or pronoun and answer one of the following questions:

- Which one?
- What kind?
- How many/much?
- Whose?

A young lawyer from Albuquerque disappeared last night.

The prepositional phrase "from Albuquerque" is an adjective describing the subject, *lawyer*, and answers the question "Which lawyer?"

> I would like two vanilla cupcakes with chocolate frosting.

The prepositional phrase "with chocolate frosting" is an adjective describing *cupcakes*, and it answers the question "What kind of cupcakes?"

Prepositional Phrases as Adverbs

In a sentence, prepositional phrases can function as adverbs. Adverbs describe verbs, adjectives, or other adverbs. However, prepositional phrases acting as adverbs will *only* describe verbs.

They will answer the same questions as regular adverbs:

- When?
- Where?
- Why?
- How?
- How often?

> Marcus asked the Kia dealership for a replacement part.

In this sentence, the prepositional phrase "for a replacement part" is an adverb; it describes the verb *asked* and answers the question "Why?"

> Every morning, I take a walk around my apartment complex.

In this sentence, the prepositional phrase "around my apartment complex" is an adverb describing *walk* and answering the question "Where?"

Prepositions will always be part of a prepositional phrase. A word that looks like a preposition but does not appear inside a prepositional phrase is probably a regular adverb.

Prepositional Phrase	The hikers were found over twenty miles into the forest.
Adverb	Do you want to stay over?

11g Conjunctions

Conjunctions connect words or groups of words. There are three main types of conjunctions:

- Coordinating conjunctions
- Correlative conjunctions
- Subordinating conjunctions

Coordinating Conjunctions

Coordinating conjunctions join closely related words or groups of words together. Use the acronym FANBOYS to remember the seven coordinating conjunctions:

F	A	N	B	O	Y	S
For	And	Nor	But	Or	Yet	So

Coordinating conjunctions have three main functions:

- Joining two or more words
- Joining word groups
- Joining independent clauses

Joining Two or More Words

Coordinating conjunctions can join two or more words, such as nouns, adjectives, adverbs, or verbs.

Nouns	Emily and Cassandra were eager to compete against each other.
Adjectives	During the tour, we saw manatees in the clear and sparkling water.
Adverbs	The oak tree's leaves fell suddenly and unexpectedly only two weeks into autumn.
Verbs	The results of the study both surprised and worried the team of scientists.

Joining Word Groups

Coordinating conjunctions can join word groups, such as prepositional phrases.

> This morning, we walked on the beach and under the pier.

> The dog's toy is probably under the bed or behind the sofa.

Joining Independent Clauses

Coordinating conjunctions can join two or more independent clauses. Independent clauses are independent because they can stand alone as complete sentences. They contain a subject, a verb, and a complete thought.

> The boys tried to catch the lamp before it hit the floor, but they were too late.

When joining two independent clauses with a coordinating conjunction, always use a comma. The comma should be placed at the end of the first clause and before the conjunction.

> Eating is one of my favorite activities, but eating while reading is even better.

> The park closes after sunset, so we need to leave in an hour.

Correlative Conjunctions

Correlative conjunctions, like coordinating conjunctions, join closely related words or word groups together. However, they always appear in pairs.

both, and	neither, nor
either, or	whether, or
not only, but also	

Both Sofia Vergara and Eric Stonestreet were nominated for Golden Globe awards.

We can ship your order to either your home or your local retailer.

That claim is neither valid, nor relevant to this debate.

Whether traveling for work or sitting on your couch, you can access your music easily.

Subordinating Conjunctions

Subordinating conjunctions introduce dependent clauses. A dependent clause is a word group that does not express a complete thought even though it contains a subject and/or verb. Here are some of the most common subordinating conjunctions.

after	if
although	once
as	since
because	until
despite	when
even though	while

Take a look at this example:

Even though it rained

The subordinating conjunction "Even though" introduces the dependent clause "Even though it rained." Dependent clauses must be combined with independent clauses to form complete sentences.

> Even though it rained, we had a good time at the barbecue.

> Sarah stayed up working on her project until she fell asleep at her desk.

> Once the auditions are finished, we'll decide who gets a call-back.

11h Interjections

Interjections are words or short word groups that show emphasis or emotion. Interjections can be used in two main ways:

- Greetings
- Emphasis

Interjections as Greetings

Interjections are used as greetings in emails and letters.

> Good morning, all!

> Hi, Emily

> Dear Mr. Russell

Interjections for Emphasis

Interjections are used to emphasize words or feelings. Note that interjections for emphasis are used more in personal writing than in academic or professional writing.

> Well, this is certainly a surprise.

> Wow! You definitely need to check out the new restaurant that just opened.

Chapter 12

Components of a Complete Sentence

Complete sentences have three main characteristics:

- Capital letters and punctuation marks
- Subjects and verbs
- Complete thoughts

If a word group is missing any of these three things, it is not a complete sentence.

12a Capital Letters and Punctuation Marks

Capital Letters

Complete sentences always start with a capital letter, no matter what the first word of the sentence is.

The curtains fluttered in the open window.

Most airports have places to buy food.

Bring your favorite dessert to the party.

Punctuation Marks

Complete sentences always end with a punctuation mark. There are three types of punctuation marks for ending sentences:

Period:	The weather forecasts predicts sunshine for the whole week.
Question Mark:	Has the committee made a decision yet?
Exclamation Point:	Don't lose your ticket!

Each punctuation mark has a specific purpose.

Period

Periods end sentences that are not exclamations or questions.

Nicole sleepily brewed her first cup of coffee.

Every Wednesday, we have a staff meeting.

Question Mark

Question marks end sentences that ask direct questions.

What time are you coming home?

How many pints are in a gallon?

There's a difference between **direct** questions and **indirect** questions. Indirect questions tell the audience about a question instead of asking a question.

Direct: Where would you go if you could visit any country in the world?

Indirect: My professor asked where I would go if I could visit any country in the world.

Exclamation Point

Exclamation points end sentences that express a strong feeling or idea. Although it's common to use multiple exclamation points (or question marks) in a text or social media post, formal writing only requires one punctuation mark.

I missed you so much!

My cat is missing!

12b Subjects and Verbs

Complete sentences always contain both a subject and a verb. If a word group is missing one or both of these parts of speech, it is not a complete sentence.

Subjects

A subject is whom or what a sentence is about. Subjects are almost always nouns or pronouns.

She forgot to lock her car.

Congress has been working for months to balance the budget.

Sentences giving the audience a command or request contain an **implied** subject. An implied subject does not appear in the sentence because the speaker is talking to the audience directly.

(You) Get off the grass!   (You) Please pass
                                               the salad.

A subject will never appear inside a prepositional phrase (a group of related words that begins with a preposition).

In three minutes, the box of Girl Scout cookies was completely empty.

In this sentence, there are two prepositional phrases: "In three minutes" and "of Girl Scout Cookies." This means that the subject of the sentence is *box*.

In three minutes, the box of Girl Scout cookies was completely empty.

Verbs

Verbs are words that represent actions, relationships, or states of being. The two types of verbs are **action** and **linking**.

Action verbs show the subject doing an action.

During the rally, the crowd screamed in protest.

The huge audience intimidated Bethany.

Linking verbs connect the subject to a description.

The conventional wisdom is often wrong. (Steven D. Levitt)

The news was disappointing.

Verbs can be more than one word. This is often because of a helping verb, which changes the form of the main verb so that it grammatically fits the sentence.

On your first day, you will complete the steps in the training manual.

Because of the weather conditions, locals were forced to evacuate.

The contestants are writing memoirs for this year's competition.

Finding Subjects and Verbs

Finding the subject and verb in a sentence isn't always easy. In most sentences in the English language, subjects come before verbs, such as "The dog barks." However, some sentences place the subject after or inside the verb. This is especially common in questions.

Subject after the Verb:	"To the beaches!" exclaimed the general.
Subject inside the Verb:	"Will you run in tomorrow's race?

Both subjects and verbs can also be **compound**. Two people could be doing the same action, or one person could be doing two different actions. Compound subjects and verbs are linked by conjunctions.

Compound Subject:	*Horton Hears a Who!* and *The Cat in the Hat* are two famous books by Dr. Seuss.
Compound Verb:	As volunteers, we prepared and packaged meals for families in need.

Subject-Verb Checklist

If you are having a difficult time finding the subject and/or verb in a sentence, follow these steps:

- ✓ Put parentheses around any prepositional phrases.

- ✓ Look for an action or linking verb.

- ✓ Ask yourself whom or what is doing the action or being described.

Here's an example that uses the checklist:

(After the appointment), my mom and sister were waiting (for me) (in the lobby).

(After the appointment), my mom and sister were waiting (for me) (in the lobby).

(After the appointment), my mom and sister were waiting (for me) (in the lobby).

12c Complete Thoughts

Complete sentences always express complete thoughts. When a word group contains a complete thought, that means it is logical and finished.

Independent and Dependent Clauses

If a word group contains a subject and a verb, but does not express a complete thought, it is a dependent clause. These clauses are dependent because they can't stand alone.

Though they were running out of time.

This sentence contains a subject (*they*) and a verb ("*were running*"), but it does not express a complete thought. Therefore, it's a dependent clause. Here are a few more examples of dependent clauses:

As Caitlin smiled at the crowd of friends and family members.

When the pilot congratulated the crewmembers.

That the florist added to the bouquet at the last minute.

Notice that dependent clauses usually begin with a word that makes the rest of the sentence sound incomplete. This word is often a subordinating conjunction. If this word is removed, the sentence expresses a complete thought.

~~As~~ Caitlin smiled at the crowd of friends and family members.

~~When~~ the pilot congratulated the crewmembers.

~~That~~ the florist added to the bouquet at the last minute.

These examples are now complete sentences, or independent clauses. They are independent because they can stand alone. They start with a capital letter; end with a punctuation mark; and contain a subject, a verb, and a complete thought.

PART 4

Punctuation and Mechanics

Chapter 13

Punctuation   152

13a Commas   152
13b Unnecessary Commas   156
13c Colons   158
13d Semicolons   159
13e Apostrophes   161
13f Quotation Marks   163
13g Parentheses   166
13h Brackets   167
13i Hyphens   167
13j Ellipses   170
13k Dashes   172

Chapter 14

Spelling   174

14a Common Spelling Rules   174
14b Commonly Confused Words   178

Chapter 13

Punctuation

13a Commas

Commas organize information in sentences so that it's easy to read. Commas are used in five main ways:

- Lists
- Compound sentences
- Introductory words, phrases, and clauses
- Extra or unnecessary details
- Adjectives

Lists

If a list has more than two items, use commas to separate them.

> We are running a special on workout gear, camping equipment, and women's athletic socks.

> There are meetings about the budget, marketing, community outreach, and insurance.

In these sentences, a comma is placed after each list item. Depending on the format of your writing, you may or may not need a comma before the conjunction. In MLA format, you do need this comma. In APA format, you do not need this comma.

MLA   Could you pick up popcorn, juice, and apples from the store?

APA   Could you pick up popcorn, juice and apples from the store?

Compound Sentences

A compound sentence is made up of two independent clauses joined by a comma and a conjunction. An independent clause is a complete sentence because it contains a subject, a verb, and a complete thought.

The band sat on the south end of the stadium, and the dance team sat on the north end.

The couple invited twenty-five guests to the wedding, but at least forty people actually came.

I love warm weather and swimming, so summer is my favorite season.

Exercise

Read the compound sentences below and insert commas in the correct places.

Springtime is beautiful but my car is covered in pollen.

A week-long break is coming up so my friends and I are planning a road trip.

My aunt plays the cello and my uncle plays the guitar.

Introductory Words, Phrases, and Clauses

Introductory means "beginning," so introductory words, phrases, and clauses provide extra information at the beginning of a sentence. They are always followed by a comma. These are the three common types of introductions:

- Transition words
- Prepositional phrases
- Dependent clauses

Transition Words

Transition words show relationships between ideas. Here are some examples:

Next, gently stir the flour mixture into the batter.

However, the most successful Kickstarter campaign raised over $5 million dollars.

Then, the double agent jumped out of the helicopter and into the ocean!

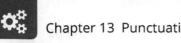

Prepositional Phrases

A prepositional phrase is a group of related words that starts with a preposition and ends with a noun or pronoun. Prepositional phrases shorter than five words, like "in two years," do not need a comma unless the sentence would be confusing without one.

> By the end of the war, over 300,000 soldiers had served overseas.

> After my little brother's piano recital, we all went out for ice cream.

> Under a pile of unfolded laundry, I finally found my missing shoe.

Dependent Clauses

A dependent clause is a word group with a subject and a verb, but it does not express a complete thought. Dependent clauses often begin with subordinating conjunctions.

> Although the movie did not win any awards, it was immensely popular.

> Once he had dinner in the oven, Joshua started preparing dessert.

> Since the music video was released, it has been viewed millions of times.

Extra or Unnecessary Details

If extra details do not change the meaning of a sentence, they should be surrounded by commas.

> Jonathan, who had slept for five hours the night before, felt exhausted.

> Jonathan felt exhausted.

There are commas before and after the extra details in the sentence above because removing those details does not change the meaning of the sentence.

If details *do* change the meaning of the sentence, they do *not* need any commas.

> The group talked about all of the people who had influenced their lives.

> The group talked about all of the people.

This sentence does not have the same meaning without the extra details, so no commas are needed. Here are a few more examples of sentences with extra or unnecessary details:

> Marie Curie, born in 1867, won multiple Nobel Prizes for her work in physics and chemistry.

> The haiku, a poem with only seventeen syllables, originated in Japan.

Adjectives

Use commas to separate similar adjectives that are describing the same noun or pronoun.

> The accident caused severe, irreversible damage to the car.

Generally, if you can insert the word *and* between two adjectives, you should use a comma to separate them.

> The speech about the former principal was a genuine and heartfelt tribute.

> The speech about the former principal was a genuine, heartfelt tribute.

Here are a few more examples:

> My impetuous, excitable sister cannot sit still.

> The bright, gaudy lights of the city were visible from the airplane.

13b Unnecessary Commas

Essential Details

If a sentence contains details that are essential to the meaning of the sentence, no commas are needed.

> The play had an intermission, that was twenty minutes long.

The word group "that was twenty minutes long" is essential to the meaning of the sentence. Without it, the audience does not receive any information about the intermission. Therefore, a comma is not needed.

Here are a few more examples:

> Corban knew immediately, what his decision would be.

> The week-old baby already recognized, which voices belonged to her parents.

Dependent Clauses

A comma is not needed for a dependent clause that comes after an independent clause.

> We watched TV, because it was too rainy to go outside.

The word group "because it was too rainy to go outside" is a dependent clause; it cannot stand alone. Because of this, no comma is needed to join it to the independent clause "We watched TV."

Here are a few more examples:

> Marisol drove home, while her sister napped in the passenger seat.

> The normally busy road was empty, since it was Saturday morning.

Short Prepositional Phrases

Usually, introductory information is separated from the rest of a sentence by a comma. However, if a sentence begins with a prepositional phrase that is shorter than five words, no comma is needed unless the sentence could be confusing without it.

> After the exam, the students discussed questions they were unsure about.

"After the exam" is a prepositional phrase with fewer than five words, so no comma is needed.

Here are a few more examples:

> In ten minutes, the burgers will be ready.

> By evening, the group was restless.

First and Last List Items

While commas are needed between three or more items in a list, commas are not necessary before or after a list.

> My girlfriend's favorite musical genres are, rock, electronica, and jazz.

> Most people think tomatoes, beans, and peanuts, are vegetables.

Exercise

Read the sentences below and cross out any unnecessary commas.

In August, they are moving into a new apartment.

Remember, hang the banner on the wall, that is across from the door.

Breakfast, lunch, and dinner, are provided by the company.

The airport is more crowded than usual, since Christmas is next week.

13c Colons

Colons have four main uses:

- Lists
- Salutations
- Quotations
- Related numbers

Lists

Colons can be used to introduce a list.

> The travel agency offered five destinations: Houston, Detroit, Panama City, Orlando, and Portland.

> We watched three movies in my "Modern Superheroes" film class last week: *The Avengers*, *The Dark Knight*, and *The Lego Movie*.

A colon that introduces a list must come after a complete sentence, not a dependent clause.

> *good numbers*
> During his professional baseball career, David Smith had ∧:
>
> thirty-four home runs, twenty-nine doubles, and six All-Star
>
> Game appearances.

Salutations

A salutation is a phrase that greets a person or group. Using a colon after a salutation is most common in professional writing.

> Dear Ms. Ladson:
>
> To the Human Resources Department:
>
> Hello all:

Quotations

Colons can be used instead of commas to introduce quotations.

> John Steinbeck made the following statement: "I hate cameras. They are so much more sure than I am about everything."

Similar to lists, the colon must follow a complete sentence, not a dependent clause.

Correct	Consider the words of Nelson Mandela: "I like friends who have independent minds because they tend to make you see problems from all angles."
Incorrect	Nelson Mandela said: "I like friends who have independent minds because they tend to make you see a problem from all angles."

Related Numbers

Colons join related numbers. Take a look at these examples:

Purpose	Examples
Journal issues	*Field and Stream* 24:5, *Journal of American Psychology* 36:2
Religious texts	Quran 27:79, Philippians 3:20
Ratios	1:3, 5:4
Times	3:05 p.m., 11:59 a.m.

13d Semicolons

Semicolons have two primary uses:

- Combining independent clauses
- Separating long list items

Combining Independent Clauses

Use a semicolon to combine two independent clauses into one sentence. Independent clauses—also called complete sentences—can stand alone, but if they're closely related, using a semicolon will connect them.

Greg drives like a maniac. His girlfriend is always asking him to slow down.

Greg drives like a maniac; his girlfriend is always asking him to slow down.

To make sure you're using a semicolon correctly, try separating the halves into different sentences.

Correct	Incorrect
I love milk and cookies; they remind me of visiting my grandmother.	I love milk and cookies; because they remind me of visiting my grandmother.
I love milk and cookies. They remind me of visiting my grandmother.	I love milk and cookies. Because they remind me of visiting my grandmother.

Separating Long List Items

Normally, commas separate each item in a list. However, if those items are long and contain commas, using semicolons will prevent confusion.

With Commas — The store had juicy, green apples, crisp, fresh pears, ripe, yellow bananas, and both green and red, seedless, firm grapes.

With Semicolons — The store had juicy, green apples; crisp, fresh pears; ripe, yellow bananas; and both green and red, seedless, firm grapes.

In the list that uses semicolons, the items are more clearly separated and defined. Here are a few more examples.

During the tour, the band stopped in Kansas City, Missouri; Seattle, Washington; and Sacramento, California.

For dinner, we had chicken, with lemon and pepper; mashed potatoes, with garlic, butter, and sour cream; and steamed green beans.

13e Apostrophes

Apostrophes are used in three common situations:

- Possessive nouns
- Contractions
- Shortened numbers and words

Possessive Nouns

A possessive noun shows ownership of an item. These nouns always use an apostrophe.

The jury's decision shocked everyone in the courtroom.

In tomorrow's game, be sure to wear your ankle brace.

Devon's room is always cleaner than mine.

To make a singular noun possessive, add an apostrophe and the letter *s*.

The cat's favorite scratching post is my leg.

Check the restaurant's website for meal specials.

If a singular noun already ends in *s*, there are two options. Some writers add an apostrophe and an extra *s*. Others simply add an apostrophe.

Dr. Deidre James's lecture was about the history of genetic science.

Dr. Deidre James' lecture was about the history of genetic science.

If a plural noun doesn't end with *s*, make it possessive by adding an apostrophe and the letter *s*.

He cares too much about other people's opinions.

The children's birthdays are all in the spring.

If a plural noun does end in *s*, simply add an apostrophe.

All of the candidates' families attended the debate.

The tourists' faces were sunburned but happy.

Exercise

Next to each word below, write the possessive version.

pancake　　_____

mice　　_____

games　　_____

faces　　_____

geese　　_____

Contractions

Contract means "to draw together" or "become smaller." Contractions are phrases that have been shortened into one word. Contractions use apostrophes to mark the spot where one or more letters have been removed. For example, when "has not" becomes *hasn't*, the apostrophe marks the spot where the letter *o* used to be.

Here is a list of common contractions.

Phrase	Contraction
let us	let's
cannot	can't
she is	she's
they are	they're
has not	hasn't
it is	it's
he will	he'll
who is	who's
will not	won't

Remember, most of the time formal academic writing should not contain contractions.

Shortened Numbers and Words

Similar to contractions, shortened numbers and words use apostrophes to replace letters or numbers. Take a look at these common examples.

Long Version	Shortened Version
of the clock	o'clock
hanging out	hangin' out
madam	ma'am
1990s	'90s

13f Quotation Marks

Quotation marks prevent confusion because they visually set apart words or groups of words. Quotation marks are most commonly used in the following situations:

- Quoting
- Titles of articles, short stories, and chapters

Basics of Quotation Marks

Quotation marks always come in pairs.

Correct	"I've been busy baking," my roommate, Julie, replied with a sigh.
Incorrect	"I've been busy baking, my roommate, Julie, replied with a sigh.

Periods, commas, exclamation points, and question marks that appear at the end of a quote should be placed inside the closing quotation mark.

The author argues that people prefer fast food to homemade meals because "convenient and affordability are their highest priorities."

Zach asked, "How many months will the program last?"

"Changing our return policy will negatively impact our customers," the associate argued.

If an entire sentence is a question or exclamation, put the punctuation mark outside of the quotation marks.

I can't believe you've never read "The Gift of the Magi"!

Are we supposed to read the chapter "Social Experiments"?

Exercise

Use the guidelines above to add a punctuation mark and a closing quotation mark to the ends of the following sentences.

Have you read the article called "My Week in the Desert

His instructor said, "For extra credit, attend the festival on Saturday

"If you give me a ride," my sister said, "I'll buy you lunch

Quotes

The most common use of quotation marks is to indicate when someone else's words are being repeated. This is also called **quoting**.

The manager said, "Remember to check all parts of the store before closing at night."

According to the U.S. Department of Education website, "Eighteen percent of all ninth graders complete four-year degrees within ten years."

In both of these examples, the exact words of a source is being repeated. Notice that a comma is placed before the quote because it's a complete sentence.

Quotes can also be just a few words. In these cases, a comma before the quoted word(s) is usually unnecessary.

In a recent review, a food critic called the Indigo Grill "offensive to anyone with taste buds."

T.S. Eliot said that plays "should give you something to think about."

Titles

Quotation marks are used around the titles of the following works:

- Articles
- Short stories
- Book chapters

Here are a few examples:

Article	For the school magazine, I wrote an article called "The Five People You Meet on Campus."
Short Story	F. Scott Fitzgerald's "Bernice Bobs Her Hair" is a humorous tale that ends with two unplanned haircuts.
Book Chapter	In Chapter 2, "Climate Change and Controversy," the author explores arguments from three different perspectives.

Single Quotation Marks

Use single quotation marks to indicate a quote or title within another quote.

The lifeguard explained, "I heard her yelling 'Someone get help!' and ran to see what was going on."

"As part of tonight's assignment," stated Professor Bering, "you will be writing a one-page response to 'Hills Like White Elephants' by Ernest Hemingway."

13g Parentheses

Basics of Parentheses

Parentheses always come in pairs.

> After my ancestors emigrated from Georgia (the country, not the state), they settled in West Virginia.

Punctuation marks should be placed after and outside of the closing parenthesis.

| Incorrect | Once the reports are submitted, (and approved) we can dedicate our time to planning. |
| Correct | Once the reports are submitted (and approved), we can dedicate our time to planning. |

If the information inside the parentheses forms a complete sentence, the punctuation mark can go inside the closing parenthesis.

> This year, I'm going to bring a sweatshirt to the homecoming game. (Kick-off is scheduled for 6 p.m., and it gets cold in the evenings.)

Parenthetical Information

Parentheses are used to add interesting or nonessential information to a sentence, such as dates, illustrations, or comments. These details are called parenthetical information.

> Henry VIII (1491-1547) ruled England for almost forty years.

> I love going to South Beach (in Miami, Florida) with my cousins.

Abbreviations

Parentheses introduce abbreviations the first time they appear in a piece of writing. Afterwards, the abbreviation does not need parentheses.

My roommate wants to work for the World Health Organization (WHO).

This drug has not been approved by the Food and Drug Administration (FDA). The FDA released a report this morning with warnings about possible side effects.

13h Brackets

Inside Parentheses

Use brackets to add extra details to information that is already inside parentheses.

My brother watches all of the major league sports (except the National Basketball Association [NBA]).

All of the dogs at the show were purebred (except for Spark the Labradoodle [Labradoodles are Labrador-poodle mixes]).

Inside Quotation Marks

Use brackets to add extra information to text inside quotation marks.

Colbie said, "I love it."

Colbie said, "I love [my new car]."

The quote in the first sentence is not clear on what *it* is. Using brackets to add information clarifies the meaning.

Robert Brault said, "If it is unexpressed, it is plain, old-fashioned ingratitude."

Robert Brault said, "If [gratitude] is unexpressed, it is plain, old-fashioned ingratitude."

13i Hyphens

Hyphens link together two words or word parts. They are most commonly used in the following situations:

- Compound nouns
- Compound adjectives
- Numbers
- Words with prefixes

Compound Nouns

Compound nouns are nouns made up of two or more words. Some compound nouns are linked together with hyphens. Here are a few examples:

mother-in-law   merry-go-round

two-year-old   goody-goody

Unfortunately, there's no quick and easy trick for knowing when a compound noun is hyphenated, so if you're unsure, use a dictionary to check your spelling.

Compound Adjectives

Compound adjectives are two or more words that are being used to describe the same noun or pronoun.

The star-studded cast included all of my favorite celebrities.

Andrew felt like he was having a quarter-life crisis.

In these examples, both of the words that form the compound adjective are essential. *Star-studded* is describing *cast*, and *quarter-life* is describing *crisis*. If you removed one of the words, the adjective wouldn't make sense.

The studded cast included all of my favorite celebrities.

Andrew felt like he was having a quarter crisis.

Exercise

Read the word groups below and add a hyphen between the compound adjectives.

> a life size teddy bear
>
> the purring black cat
>
> the green eyed monster
>
> a delicious pumpkin pie

Numbers

Use hyphens to spell out fractions and numbers between twenty-one and ninety-nine. No hyphen is needed in numbers like one hundred or three thousand.

thirty-five	one-half
one hundred and eighty-two	two thousand and fifty-five
seventy-one	six-tenths

Words with Prefixes

Prefixes are word parts added to the beginning of a word in order to create a new word. Hyphens join prefixes to words.

> The ex-teacher used his experiences in the classroom as the basis for his novel.

> Most cameras include a self-timer function.

Hyphens are also used for prefixes when the spelling of the word is potentially confusing.

> The careful re-creation of the destroyed monument took archaeologists over ten years.

In this sentence, *re-creation* means "creating something again." Without a hyphen, this word might be confused with *recreation*, which means "activity."

Here are some more words that would be confusing or unclear without a hyphen:

de-ice   anti-American

re-enter   all-inclusive

post-WWI   re-sign

13j Ellipses

Basics of Ellipses

Ellipses are made up of three periods in a row. They show that information has been removed from a quotation.

Original	One of the survey participants said, "I don't think this new phone, with all of its bells and whistles, is any better than the phone I use currently."
Revised	One of the survey participants said, "I don't think this new phone . . . is any better than the phone I use currently."

Using Ellipses

When using ellipses, never take out information in a way that changes the meaning of the original quote.

Original	John Louis von Neumann stated, "If people do not believe that mathematics is simple, it is only because they do not realize how complicated life is."
Correct Revision	John Louis von Neumann stated, "If people do not believe that mathematics is simple . . . they do not realize how complicated life is."
Incorrect Revision	John Louis von Neumann stated, "People . . . believe . . . mathematics is simple."

Make sure fragments or confusing sentences are not created by using an ellipsis. The overall structure of the quotation should still make sense.

Correct	Sonia Sotomayor said, "In every position that I've been in, there have been naysayers . . . who don't believe I can do the work."
Incorrect	Sonia Sotomayor said, "In every position that I've been in . . . who don't believe I can do the work."

Formatting Ellipses

Add spaces before and after an ellipsis, as well as between each of the periods.

Correct	"The Henkel Corporation is committed to . . . superior customer service."
Incorrect	"The Henkel Corporation is committed to... superior customer service."

Ellipses are not required at the beginning or end of a quotation.

Correct	Winston Churchill said, "You have enemies? Good. That means you've stood up for something."
Incorrect	Winston Churchill said, "You have enemies? Good. That means you've stood up for something . . ."

If an ellipsis comes immediately after another punctuation mark, keep both.

Original	Edmund Burke said, "Hypocrisy can afford to be magnificent in its promises, for never intending to go beyond promise, it costs nothing."
Revision	Edmund Burke said, "Hypocrisy can afford to be magnificent in its promises, . . . it costs nothing."

13k Dashes

Dashes are lines slightly longer than hyphens. They are sometimes called "em-dashes" because they are about the same length as a lowercase letter *m*. Dashes have two primary uses:

- Add extra details
- Add emphasis

Add Extra Details

Similar to commas, dashes can be used to add extra details to a sentence. However, dashes should be used when information being added to a sentence already contains commas.

> The Fantastic Four—Mr. Fantastic, the Invisible Girl, the Human Torch, and the Thing—first appeared in a comic book in 1961.

> The tour destinations—Covent Garden, Trafalgar Square, and the Houses of Parliament—are within reasonable walking distance of each other.

Add Emphasis

Dashes also give greater emphasis to extra information because a dash signals a longer pause to the reader than a comma.

> The full impact of the loss—all $100,000 of it—did not yet seem real.

> The remains of King Richard III—lost for over five hundred years—were found in 2012 under a parking lot.

Formatting Dashes

To create a dash in a typed document, type two hyphens back-to-back. Many programs will automatically turn the hyphens into a dash. However, using two hyphens is also acceptable.

Do not add spaces before or after a dash.

Correct   My two favorite professors—Dr. Martingdale and Dr. Lee—were kind enough to write me letters of recommendation.

Incorrect My two favorite professors — Dr. Martingdale and Dr. Lee — were kind enough to write me letters of recommendation.

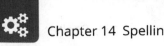

Chapter 14

Spelling

Spelling makes a big impression in school, at work, and in everyday life. Spelling a word wrongly, or using the wrong word altogether, can make your writing seem careless or untrustworthy.

14a Common Spelling Rules

There are three common situations that have specific spelling rules:

- *IE* and *EI*
- Plural words
- Suffixes

IE and EI

"*I* before *E*, except after *C* or in words like *neighbor* or *weigh*." Usually, this rule is true. Here a few examples:

I Before *E*	Except after *C*	Or in Words Like *Weigh*
achieve	ceiling	weight
believe	deceit	their
brief	perceive	sleigh
relief	receipt	vein
retrieve		

Some words are exceptions to the "*I* before *E* rule."

- Use *ie* after the *–sh* sound
- Use *ei* if the vowels are pronounced like the *i* in *bit*
- Use *ei* in weird words

Use *ie* after the *-sh* sound	Use *ei* for words like *bit*	Use *ei* in weird words
ancient	foreign	neither
patient	forfeit	either
species		weird

Plural Words

When words are made plural, the spelling of their endings often changes.

If a word ends in any of the following letters, add *–es* to make it plural.

-s	-sh	-ch	-x	-z

If a word ends in any other letter, add *–s* to make it plural.

-es	*-s*
box → boxes	assignment → assignments
brush → brushes	caterpillar → caterpillars
church → churches	nap → naps
hoax → hoaxes	phone → phones
maze → mazes	straw → straws

When words that end in *–o* become plural, they end either with *–es* or *–s*. There's no easy way to remember which *–o* words have a certain ending, so if you're not sure about the correct spelling, check a dictionary.

-es	*-s*
echo → echoes	combo → combos
hero → heroes	logo → logos
potato → potatoes	taco → tacos
tomato → tomatoes	typo → typos
veto → vetoes	video → videos

Some words are **irregular**. This means that instead of adding *–es* or *–s* to the end, you need to change the spelling of the word itself. For example, the plural of *foot* is not *foots*, it's *feet*.

Here are a few more examples of irregular words:

- child → children
- goose → geese
- mouse → mice
- person → people
- tooth → teeth

Other words are spelled the same whether they are singular or plural. For example, the plural of *aircraft* is still *aircraft*.

Here are a few more examples of words that are spelled the same whether they're singular or plural:

- deer
- elk
- fish
- sheep
- species

Suffixes

Suffixes are word parts added to the end of a root in order to change the meaning. For example, *standard* is a root that means "normal." The suffix *–ize* means "make like." Combining them creates the word *standardize*, which means "to make normal."

Suffixes affect the spelling of a word in three situations:

- Silent E words
- Final Y words
- Final consonants

Silent E

If you are adding a suffix that starts with a **vowel**, drop the silent *e* at the end of the word.

Word	+	Suffix	=	New Word
advise	+	ing	=	advising
dance	+	ing	=	dancing
excite	+	able	=	excitable
file	+	ed	=	filed
narrate	+	ion	=	narration

If you are adding a suffix that starts with a **consonant**, keep the silent *e*.

Word	+	Suffix	=	New Word
advertise	+	ment	=	advertisement
home	+	ward	=	homeward
hope	+	ful	=	hopeful
safe	+	ty	=	safety
state	+	ment	=	statement

If dropping the silent *e* could cause confusion between two words, keep the silent e and add the suffix. For example, to add the suffix *–ing* to the word *dye*, as in "I love tie-dyeing shirts," spell it *dyeing* so that it will not be confused with *dying*.

Final Y

When the letter before the final *e* is a vowel, simply add the suffix to the end of the word

Word	+	Suffix	=	New Word
attorney	+	s	=	attorneys
employ	+	er	=	employer
enjoy	+	ing	=	enjoying

When the letter before the final *e* is a consonant, change the *y* to an *i* before adding the suffix.

Word	+	Suffix	=	New Word
easy	+	ly	=	easily
try	+	s	=	tries
mystery	+	ous	=	mysterious

The suffix *–ing* is an exception to this rule. Always keep the final *y* when adding *–ing*.

Word	+	Suffix	=	New Word
bury	+	ing	=	burying
carry	+	ing	=	carrying
rely	+	ing	=	relying

Final Consonants

If a one-syllable word ends with *consonant-vowel-consonant,* like *sit,* double the final consonant before adding the suffix. A **syllable** is the basic unit of a word's pronunciation. For example, *flip* has one syllable while *poster* has two syllables.

Word	+	Suffix	=	New Word
beg	+	ing	=	begging
hot	+	er	=	hotter
hop	+	ed	=	hopped

If a multiple-syllable word ends in *consonant-vowel-consonant* and the stress is placed on the last syllable, like *submit,* double the final consonant before adding a suffix. *Stress* means emphasis, either written or spoken.

Word	+	Suffix	=	New Word
begin	+	ing	=	beginning
control	+	ed	=	controlled
forbid	+	en	=	forbidden

14b Commonly Confused Words

These words are commonly confused because they sound alike and are spelled similarly.

Accept and Except

Accept is a verb that means "to receive something."

Due to budget concerns, the committee decided not to accept the proposal.

I will accept the promotion if it's offered.

Except is a preposition that means "excluding" or "leaving out."

The tornado hit all of the county except Mount Pleasant.

He likes all pizza toppings except olives.

Affect and Effect

Affect is a verb that means "to change or influence."

The crowd was deeply affected by the news.

Every vote affects the outcome of an election.

Effect is a noun that means "a consequence or result."

Painting the wall orange had a dramatic effect on the room's appearance.

The special effects in the movie won an award.

Choose and Chose

Choose is a verb that means "to select something."

Mindy chooses the layout for every article in the magazine.

It's impossible for many people to choose just one favorite book.

Chose, with just one *o*, is the past tense form of *choose*.

At dinner yesterday, I was shocked that Raul chose ice cream instead of cheesecake for dessert.

Damian chose to write about nuclear energy for his final paper.

Its and It's

Its is a possessive pronoun.

The parrot turned its head and squawked loudly.

That car needs its windshield cleaned.

It's is a contraction formed from the phrase "it is."

It's almost 2:00 p.m. and she is still in bed.

My favorite kind of weather is when it's sunny and 65 degrees Fahrenheit.

Loose and Lose

Loose is an adjective that means "not tight."

This handle is loose; it comes off every time I open the drawer.

After nine weeks of working out, my clothing started to feel loose.

Lose is a verb that means "to fail a competition" or "to misplace something."

If the Rockets lose tonight's game, they will not advance to the playoffs.

He is constantly losing his keys.

Past and Passed

Past is a noun that refers to time that has already happened.

The two enemies were not willing to forget the past.

In the past, she has always been polite.

Passed can either be an adjective or a past-tense verb that means "handing an item to someone" or "receiving an acceptable score."

Malaria is passed to humans through contact with mosquitos.

Lily was thrilled when she passed her math test.

Than and Then

Than is a subordinating conjunction used for comparisons.

> I am taller than my dad.

> The judges could not decide if one chef's meal was better than the other's.

Then is an adverb that shows time or order.

> Clear two more tables, and then you can take a break.

> Malique finished her essay; then, she went to the gym.

Their, They're, and There

Their is a possessive pronoun.

> Their opinion on the matter is completely uninformed.

> The research team is publishing their research soon.

They're is a contraction formed from the phrase "they are."

> They're going to get tickets to the football game.

> After dinner, they're seeing a movie.

There is an adverb that refers to a specific place.

> You can leave your shoes over there.

> There are over twenty-five corporations headquartered in Morrisville, Indiana.

Too, To, and Two

Too is an adverb that means "also."

> After Emmett got a tattoo, his brother did too.

> Too many people tried getting on the elevator, and the doors wouldn't close.

To is a preposition used to show direction.

Please send a copy of your driver's license to the Human Resources department.

My friends and I are going to the park after work.

Two **is an adjective that represents the number.**

I'd like two chocolate doughnuts.

We have two hours until the store closes.

Whether and Weather

Whether **is a subordinating conjunction used to indicate two choices.**

My roommate isn't sure whether or not she wants to join the dance team.

Whether you choose Friday or Thursday, we have openings on both days.

Weather **is a noun that represents the climate of an area.**

The National Weather Service thinks that Tropical Storm Kelly will make landfall tonight.

They want to move somewhere with warmer weather.

Whose and Who's

Whose **is a possessive pronoun.**

Whose textbook is on the desk?

The instructor remembered whose papers would be late.

Who's **is a contraction formed from the phrase "who is."**

Who's going to the concert next week?

I don't know who's presenting in class today.

Your and You're

Your is a possessive pronoun.

> Your dog is adorable.

> Kaley is buying your lunch tomorrow.

You're is a contraction formed from the phrase "you are."

> You're invited to a going-away party.

> If you don't take advantage of this opportunity, you're going to regret it.

Chapter 15

The Research Process

Often, the word *research* makes people think of school. However, research simply means "looking for information." Every day, people conduct research by looking up directions, browsing websites, reading movie reviews, or checking the weather app on their phones.

When you're writing a paper or report, research enables you to explore your topic, support your ideas, and establish your credibility as an author.

15a Making a Research Plan

Most of the time, researching involves looking for sources of information, like websites, articles, and books. Making a research plan before you begin searching will help you find the information you need more efficiently.

Research Plan Checklist

Use the following four steps to create a research plan:

- ✅ Consider your guidelines and purpose
- ✅ Conduct preliminary research
- ✅ Think about different research methods
- ✅ Schedule a research timeline

Guidelines and Purpose

At work or in school, the guidelines of your assignment are determined by your supervisor or instructor. The first step of your research plan is to carefully review these guidelines. They will affect what you research and how much you research. For example, a professor may ask you to use only scholarly sources in your paper. A supervisor may require you to use at least five sources in a presentation to your coworkers.

Once you know the guidelines of your assignment, identify your purpose. What is your goal? This determines the role of your research.

Here are some examples of how research changes depending on the purpose:

Purpose	Research
To inform the audience about the mission of the Peace Corps	Facts from the Peace Corps organization
	Anecdotes and examples from people who served in the Peace Corps
To persuade the audience that cell phone use while driving is dangerous	Facts from law enforcement and government agencies
	Statistics and expert analysis from researchers
To reflect on why you want to become a doctor	Anecdotes and descriptions from your personal experiences
	Reflections on your own feelings and motivations

Preliminary Research

The second step of making a research plan is to conduct preliminary research.

Preliminary means "introductory" or "before the main part." Before you get too far in the writing and researching process, conduct preliminary research on your topic. This will indicate whether or not there is enough material to support your main idea.

There are a few quick and easy ways to do preliminary research. One is to use an online search engine like Google or Bing. Glance through the top five or ten sites that pop up in your search results. This will give you an idea of what to expect when you start researching more thoroughly.

You can also search your school or local library catalog to see what sources they have. Consider discussing your topic with a librarian if you're unsure what to look for.

If you cannot find at least two or three sources during your preliminary research, consider adjusting your topic or main idea. It may be too specific or too broad.

Research Methods

The third step of making a research plan to decide on the best research methods. There are three common research methods:

- Library catalogs and databases
- Internet searches
- Field research

Some research methods will fit a topic better than others. Here are some examples of topics, the best research methods, and the reason why that's the best fit.

Topic	Research Method	Reason
Causes of cerebral palsy	Library catalogs/ databases	Will need books and articles written by experts
Speech-giving tactics of politicians	Internet searches	Will need video clips of political speeches
Healthy food choices on campus	Field research	Will need interviews with students and faculty

For some topics, it will work best to use multiple research methods in order to gather all the sources and information you need.

Schedule a Research Timeline

Once you have considered your guidelines and purpose, conducted preliminary research, and thought about different research methods, create a timeline to keep yourself on track. This is the fourth step of making a research plan. Knowing exactly how much time you have and how much time you'll need to spend on research is always helpful and will prevent last-minute searching.

Your research may involve planning your own schedule and considering someone else's, like if you need to meet with a librarian or conduct an interview with a student. Keeping track of these appointments on your timeline will help you use your time wisely.

Schedule dedicated "research time" so that you're less likely to procrastinate or fall behind. Sometimes, instructors have research deadlines; if so, record these in your timeline as well.

Finally, if your campus has a Writing Center, consider making an appointment to discuss your research ideas. Getting a second opinion can help you find ideas you may have missed.

15b Identifying Types of Sources

For research assignments, outside sources usually explain and/or support the author's ideas. However, not all sources are the same. Some sources work better than others in certain situations.

There are two primary ways to categorize sources:

- Primary or Secondary
- Popular or Scholarly

You can use these categories to choose the best sources for your writing.

Primary vs. Secondary Sources

Primary sources are authored or created by an original source. Some examples are original documents, first-hand accounts, speeches, research findings, and works of art.

Here are a few specific examples:

Primary Source	Examples
Original documents	The Declaration of Independence *The Secret Life of Bees* by Sue Monk Kidd
First-hand accounts	An interview with a plane crash survivor Video footage of the Normandy Invasion
Speeches	"I Have a Dream" by Martin Luther King "Ain't I A Woman" by Sojourner Truth
Research findings	Average SAT scores in 2015 Results of a sociology experiment
Works of art	"Bohemian Rhapsody" by Queen *Girl with a Pearl Earring* by Johannes Vermeer

Primary sources are useful because they allow you to get as close as possible to the source of information. You can then draw your own conclusions about how that information supports the purpose of your paper.

Secondary sources discuss information from a primary source, so the information that a secondary source discusses is not original to that source. Here are some examples:

- Newspaper articles
- Research papers
- Websites
- Documentaries

Just like rumors change as they pass from person to person, some secondary sources may be inaccurate or untrustworthy if they are too far from the original.

However, secondary sources are useful when you don't have access to the primary source. For example, you may not able to find original research on the genetic causes of diabetes, but you can use articles written by experts about this research.

Here are a few examples of secondary sources compared to primary sources:

Primary	Secondary
A survey of college students who use Snapchat	A research paper on social media apps
A commencement address by Steve Jobs	A news report about Steve Jobs' commencement address
Roll of Thunder, Hear My Cry by Mildred D. Taylor	A paper discussing themes in *Roll of Thunder, Hear My Cry* by Mildred D. Taylor
The Mayflower Compact	A website about American colonial documents
A study on poverty in Sri Lanka	An article about reducing poverty in Sri Lanka
An interview with Jimmy Fallon	A documentary about late-night television

Exercise

Read the following list and circle the secondary sources.

Samuel Pepys' diary

A newspaper article about voting

An analysis of Emily Dickinson's poetry

Breakfast at Tiffany's by Truman Capote

Popular vs. Scholarly Sources

Popular sources have been written for the general public. Sometimes, the authors of these sources are experts in their fields, while other times they are not.

Here are some examples of popular sources:

Popular Source	Examples
Books	*Yes Please* by Amy Poehler *The Hunger Games* by Suzanne Collins
Magazines	*TIME Magazine* *Entertainment Weekly*
Movies	*Star Wars: The Force Awakens* directed by J.J. Abrams *Straight Outta Compton* directed by F. Gary Gray
Newspapers	The *New York Times* The *Guardian*
Websites	*The Poetry Foundation* *Buzzfeed*

Scholarly sources are usually academic journals that contain articles written and peer-reviewed by experts in a particular field. Here are a few examples:

Journal of Soil and Water Conservation

American Journal of Psychology

Journal of Modern Literature

Journal of English Linguistics

The **purpose** and **audience** of your writing will determine if you should use popular or scholarly sources. If you are writing for an audience of experts, you should probably use scholarly sources. If you are writing for the general public, you should probably use popular sources.

There are a few major differences between popular and scholarly sources:

- Appearance and length
- Intended audience
- Author expertise
- Peer review

Appearance and Length

Scholarly sources are usually longer and more complex than popular sources. A scholarly article might also include charts and data tables, as well as a large bibliography or works cited list.

Intended Audience

Scholarly articles are specific to a particular field of study that is usually mentioned in the name of the academic journal. They use technical terms that would not appear in a popular source. Because the information in popular sources is written for the general public, the writing style is less formal than in scholarly articles.

Author Expertise

The author of a scholarly text is always an expert in an industry or field of study, while the author of a popular text may or may not be. Often, the information in a popular source is written by a journalist who has researched the topic.

Peer Review

Scholarly articles are almost always reviewed by other experts. This means that a group of respected scholars and researchers approved the content. This review process is not required for all popular sources.

Exercise

Read the following list and circle the popular sources.

Reddit

Bossypants by Tina Fey

An article in *The Journal of Nutrition*

Journal of Gender Studies

15c Finding Sources

Preliminary research can give you an idea of how many sources you can expect to find about your topic. As you begin conducting more thorough research, you should choose which research method(s) best fit your topic. These are the three most common research methods:

- Library catalogs and databases
- Internet searches
- Field research

Use one or a combination of these methods to find the sources you need.

Library Catalogs and Databases

To find books and academic journals, search the library's catalog and research databases or visit in person. **Academic journals** are scholarly sources that contain articles written and peer-reviewed by researchers or other experts in a particular field. **Research databases** are websites that allow you to search for articles from hundreds of academic journals.

If you're having trouble on your own, consider meeting with a librarian for assistance.

Internet Searches

To find websites, news articles, videos, and images, the internet is usually the best source. Conducting online research is an excellent way to find source material on rapidly changing topics like technology and pop culture. Because nearly anyone can create content online, remember to carefully evaluate each source's credibility, or believability.

Field Research

Field research involves being "in the field" collecting information through interviews and surveys. Your experience in a topic and your access to participants may limit your opportunities for field research. However, this can be an excellent way to gain information about issues that affect your local area or peers.

15d Evaluating Source Credibility

Credible means "believable" and "trustworthy." When you use credible sources, your writing will be more believable and trustworthy. However, using sources that aren't credible will make *your* writing less credible too.

Credibility Checklist

To make sure your audience believes and trusts both you and your sources, use the following four steps to identify a credible research source:

- ✓ Look for potential bias in the information
- ✓ Make sure the information is relevant
- ✓ Check the credentials of the author or organization
- ✓ Research the credibility of source material

Look for Potential Bias

Bias is a term used to describe a person's opinions and preferences. Although there's nothing wrong with having an opinion, and all authors are biased in some way, a credible author will keep his or her writing as straightforward and honest as possible.

There are three particular areas of a text that are good indications
of bias:

- Purpose
- Tone
- Supporting details

Purpose

The **purpose** is the goal of a text. There are two common signs of a biased purpose:

Agenda: the *stated* purpose of a text isn't the *actual* purpose.	An online video claims to have tips for eating healthy, but is actually a disguised advertisement for a health food store.
Conflict of Interest: the author is associated with a particular organization or has a personal stake in a topic.	A scientific study claims that bottled water is healthier than tap water, but the study was funded by a major water bottling company.

Sources with agendas or conflicts of interest can still be useful sources as long as you are aware of possible bias and acknowledge it in your writing.

Tone

Tone is the positive, negative, or neutral attitude that an author express about a topic. This can be another indicator of bias. There are three common signs of a biased tone:

Extremely Negative Language: the author uses negative or overly-emotional language.	A newspaper article uses words like *menace* and *loser* to describe drivers with expired license plates.
Exclusive Language: disrespectful language that refers to a person's gender, ethnicity or culture, physical or mental ability, or sexual orientation.	An advertisement for a car with extra safety features uses a stereotype about women being bad drivers.

Spin: the author uses positive language to describe a negative topic or situation.	A budget report describes a bankrupt company as "slightly short of their financial goals, but ready to make a dramatic recovery."

Supporting Details

The **supporting details**, or evidence, that an author chooses to *include* or *exclude* can indicate bias. There are three indications of evidence being used in a biased way:

Inaccurate Evidence: the author uses incorrect facts or fake examples.	A dieting program invents client stories of dramatic weight loss.
Unreliable Sources: the author uses evidence from a source that is untrustworthy.	An article about how the brain forms memories uses statistics from a social media post.
Excluded Details: the author leaves out information that doesn't support his or her argument.	An essay that argues for longer prison sentences does not acknowledge any opposing perspectives.

Make Sure the Information is Relevant

The second step of evaluating a source's credibility is checking for relevance. A relevant source should have the following type of information:

- Specific
- Up-to-date

Specific

If a source has only general information, and it seems like anyone could have written it, it's probably not a relevant research source. Relevant sources will include some general information, but most of the information should be specific.

Up-to-Date

Relevant sources are usually current. However, this can change depending on the subject. There is no exact "expiration date" on a source, so carefully consider the following options:

- The type of information you need
- The subject you're writing about
- The purpose of your assignment

If you're looking for statistics, data, or research findings, look for sources published within the last five years.

If you're looking for points of view, theories, or ideas, it's often more acceptable to use older sources.

In fields of study like English literature, philosophy, mathematics, and history, sources can be very old yet still relevant. For example, modern-day scholars still refer to Plato's philosophical theories, even though he lived more than 2,000 years ago.

In subjects that are changing rapidly, like science, technology, and pop culture, look for sources updated or published within the last year.

Finally, consider your assignment's purpose. If you are showing change over time or focusing on a historical event, you will need older sources. If you are making predictions or focusing on a current event, you will need newer sources.

Check the Credentials

The author of a credible source should have professional credentials and/or personal experience.

Professional credentials include having extensive education and training in a topic. For example, surgeons have completed years of medical training, so they have better professional credentials than a first-year pre-medical student.

Personal experience doesn't always involve formal training, but it's still just as valuable. For example, an author with multiple bestsellers may not have studied writing in school, but personal experience makes him or her a credible source of information about writing books.

Research the Credibility of Source Material

A credible source will reference other credible sources.

Research studies and scholarly articles should always have a Works Cited list or a reference section. Additionally, they should properly cite summaries, paraphrases, and quotes.

Websites often include hyperlinks to other sources, and online articles should acknowledge their sources in some way.

If a source has no citations, the information may be plagiarized, unreliable, or too general. Exceptions to this are works of fiction and first-hand accounts because the author is the only source for these types of texts.

15e Organizing Research

Organizing your sources is just as important as finding them. If your research is disorganized, it will be harder to find the information you need, use it in your writing, and cite it correctly. Staying organized during the research process will save you time and energy.

Here are three helpful tools that will help you organize your research:

- Research notes
- Research journal
- Working bibliography

You can use one of these tools, or a combination of all three, to organize your research.

Research Notes

Research notes are detailed records of each source that you find. These notes will help you quickly find the information you need because they will keep it organized and all in one place. Research notes also prevent you from losing information. Instead of trying to keep a mental record of your sources, you can write them down. Finally, you can use research notes to add support to the main points of your paper or outline. This will show you how your research fits into your main idea.

You can type or handwrite your research notes; use the method that is most helpful to you. However, if you copy and paste information from your notes into your paper, be careful to use citations so that you don't commit plagiarism.

Research notes should include the following information:

- Source information, including the author, title, and publication information
- Date that you accessed or read the material
- Important information, clearly labeled as a summary, paraphrase, or quote
- Additional notes or ideas about using the material in your paper

Here's an example of an entry in a student's research notes:

Source #5

"How Genetics Influence Musical Preferences"
Author: June Renkin
Publication info: Published in *National Geographic* magazine, April 2014, on pages 14-16.
Date read: Sept. 4, 2015
Important info: **Quote** from page 15: "This discovery shows that nature and nurture work together, not apart."
Notes/ideas: This would be a good supporting detail in my second body paragraph.

Research Journal

A **research journal** is a record of the entire research process. Use a journal to write down ideas, questions, or thoughts you have, even if you're not researching at that moment. Later, you can refer back to the journal and use your entries to guide your research process.

Research journals do not have a specific format, although writing the date next to each entry is usually a good idea. You can keep a research journal on your phone or computer, or in a notebook.

Here's an example of an entry in a student's research journal:

Food Advertisement and Eating Habits

April 9th
Food advertisements that target children and adolescents
What are strategies for appealing to this age group?
How much influence does an ad have? Any scientific studies?

April 10th
Are there laws or policies about advertising to kids?

The information in a research journal may overlap with your research notes. However, research journals are more focused on your thoughts and ideas than on recording specific sources.

Working Bibliography

A working bibliography is a list of sources that you plan to use in your paper. This list will expand as you move through the research process.

You can use your working bibliography to correctly cite your sources once you begin writing. Depending on whether you're following MLA guidelines or another style, you can also use the working bibliography to more quickly create a formal Works Cited list.

Working bibliographies should include a source's title, author(s), and publication information.

Here's an example of an entry in a student's working bibliography:

4. "Promoting Public Health Through Public Art in the Digital Age"
Authors: Kilaru, Ash, Sellers, and Merchant
Publication info: *American Journal of Public Health*, Volume 104, Issue 9, 2014, p. 1633-1635

The information in a working bibliography is similar to the information in research notes, but is more focused on source information.

Chapter 16

Research Writing

Once you complete the research process, you're ready to start writing. For your research assignments, you should use each piece of information to explain and support your own perspective. By the end of the project, you'll be the author of a new source of information that others can learn from and use.

There are three major parts of research writing:

- Narrowing your research
- Avoiding plagiarism
- Integrating sources into your writing

16a Narrowing Your Research

Once you finish the research process and have a list of sources, you need to choose which sources you will use. There are several factors that affect how you will narrow your research:

- Purpose
- Audience
- Possible constraints

These factors are important to consider not just while you're narrowing your research, but also during pre-writing, drafting, and researching.

Remember, the sources you choose are not set in stone. As you begin writing, you may realize that you need to add or remove a source.

Purpose

You considered your assignment's purpose, or goal, during pre-writing. In general, research assignments usually have one or a combination of the following purposes:

- Summarize/Inform
- Argue/Persuade
- Analyze

Considering your purpose will help you determine which sources are most supportive of your writing and appropriate for the topic.

One of the best ways to narrow your research is to connect the purpose of your assignment with the purpose of your sources. For example, if your assignment is a persuasive presentation, narrow your research to sources that persuaded *you*, whether they used data or a strong argument.

If you're not sure what the purpose of a source is, think about how you used it during the research process. For example, if the purpose of your assignment is to describe the invention of the bicycle, you probably found sources that helped you understand how bicycles were made; those sources are the best ones to use in your assignment.

Take a look at the following guide for connecting your purpose with your sources.

Assignment Purpose	Source Purpose
Summarize/Inform	Explains a topic Describes an important detail
Argue/Persuade	Presents evidence for a certain perspective Opposes a certain perspective,
Analyze	Examines an idea or topic Tests a theory or answers a question

Note that both your assignment and your sources might have more than one purpose. For example, a paper that *argues* for raising the minimum wage might also *summarize* general information about minimum wages in America.

Audience

As you narrow your research, consider your audience: the people who will be reading your assignment. Connect your own audience to the intended audience of your sources by separating the sources into two groups:

- Scholarly
- Popular

Scholarly sources are written for people in a particular field. These sources tend to use more technical terms and provide less background information because the assumed audience is already familiar with the subject. In general, if your audience knows a lot about your topic, you can use sources written for a scholarly audience.

Popular sources are written for a wider audience. They tend to use simple language and provide a lot of explanation and background information because they can't assume that the audience is familiar with the topic. However, if your audience does not know a lot about your topic, they would benefit most from sources written for a popular audience.

Possible Constraints

How you narrow your research is also affected by the possible constraints of an assignment:

- Instructor guidelines
- Length of the assignment/paper
- Due date

Instructor Guidelines

Narrowing your research is affected by your instructor's requirements. Many instructors have a minimum number of sources you should use. Additionally, some instructors may ask you to use specific types of sources.

Look over the list of sources you found during the research process and make sure they fit into any guidelines your instructor provided.

Length

You may have heard the following rule for research papers: "one source per page." This is not always true. There's no guaranteed way to calculate the perfect number of sources, but generally, short papers have fewer sources than long papers.

It would not be practical to have ten sources for a three-page paper. Even if you managed to include every source, it would be an overwhelming amount of information.

On the other hand, a ten-page research paper should probably have more than one source. Otherwise, your writing won't be well-supported.

Due Date

While sources can strengthen your assignment, using them properly takes time. Carefully consider when your assignment is due as you narrow your research. If you have a month to write a paper, you'll have time to use more sources in your writing. However, if the assignment is due in three days, you should consider reducing your list of sources so that they're more manageable.

16b Avoiding Plagiarism

Whenever you use outside sources in your writing, you need to make sure there is a clear difference between your original work and the work of others. **Plagiarism** is using the words or ideas of a source without giving credit to the author.

Accidental plagiarism can be prevented during the research process by carefully recording every source and marking words and ideas that don't belong to you. Whether plagiarism is accidental or deliberate, it's taken seriously in academic, professional, and everyday situations.

Types of Plagiarism

Take a look at this statement:

> No one can make you feel inferior without your consent.

This is an example of plagiarism. The author uses the exact words of Eleanor Roosevelt: "No one can make you feel inferior without your consent." However, the author has taken credit for Eleanor Roosevelt's words by not acknowledging her as the original source.

Even if you use your own words along with the words of a source, if you don't give credit to the author, it's still plagiarism. Take a look at this example:

Original:	Her unique childhood and extensive education made her an ideal candidate for the royal court. She was able to easily mingle with the other courtiers, but she still retained a distinct individuality.
Plagiarism:	Her unique childhood, and the fact that she was well-educated, made her an ideal candidate for the court. She could socialize with the other courtiers while she retained a distinct individuality.

Finally, even if you use completely original wording, using a source's ideas without giving them credit is also plagiarism.

Original:	Nathaniel Hawthorne was reportedly ashamed of his Puritan ancestors, so much so that he changed his name. However, instead of distancing himself from them, he immortalized his connection to the Puritans when he wrote and published *The Scarlet Letter*.
Plagiarism:	Hardly any American high school student doesn't at least know about *The Scarlet Letter* by Nathaniel Hawthorne. Ironically, despite his distaste for his witch-hunting ancestors, Hawthorne will always be linked to the Puritans because of his book.

When it's Not Plagiarism

There are situations when you can use information without citing it. Below are two types of information that don't need to be cited:

- Common knowledge
- Common expressions

Common knowledge includes information that the majority of people know or that can be found in many sources. For example, the fact that the Earth orbits around the sun is common knowledge, and the fact that frogs are amphibians can be found in nearly any encyclopedia.

Common expressions include proverbs and clichés. For example, "the early bird gets the worm" is a cliché with no specific, original source.

If you're unsure whether or not you're committing plagiarism, take advantage of a plagiarism checker *before* you turn in your work, or make an appointment with a writing tutor.

It's always best to cite information too much rather than not at all. Methods of citation are covered in the next section, as well as in Chapters 17-20.

16c Integrating Sources into Your Writing

Using sources in your writing will strengthen your argument or main point and support your ideas.

There are three main ways to integrate sources into your writing:

- Summarize
- Paraphrase
- Quote

Your writing will probably use all three of these methods.

There are three important things to remember as you integrate sources into your writing:

- Connect
- Balance
- Interpret

Every time you use source information, **connect** it to the rest of your writing. Don't include a summary, paraphrase, or quote without introducing it first and then explaining how it relates to your topic.

Remember to **balance** your own words and ideas with those of your sources. Outside sources are meant to support your writing, not be a substitute for it.

Finally, go beyond re-stating your sources and **interpret** the information. Explain to your audience why each piece of information is important.

Signal Phrases and Citations

To avoid plagiarism and give credit to your sources, use signal phrases and citations.

Signal phrases are used to identify source information within a sentence. They can include the title, the author, or both. Here are some examples of signal phrases:

According to [Author],

In ["Article"], [Author] asserts

The author claims that

Data from [Author's] study shows

Try to use strong, specific verbs when possible. Remember, the verbs you use in a signal phrase indicate the source's tone as well as your own.

Weak Verbs	Strong Verbs
says	claims
believes	asserts
states	argues
	confirms
	estimates
	endorses

Signal phrases are not enough on their own. **Citations** provide more source information, but not within a sentence.

The format of citations varies depending on which research style you use. In MLA style, in-text citations appear in parentheses at the end of a sentence and contain the author's last name and the information's original page number. In CMS style, footnotes at the bottom of the page provide source information such as the title and author.

Learn more about specific citation styles in Chapters 17-20.

Summarize

A **summary** explains a large amount of information in a few sentences or words. Using summaries makes the most sense when your audience needs an overview of a topic but not specific details. Because summaries are general, they should only be used when you need to inform your audience about important background information.

When you summarize, you should use your own words to explain the information and give credit to the author using signal phrases and citations.

Remember to explain how the information relates to the main point of your paper.

Here's an example of a summary that uses a signal phrase.

> In J.R.R. Tolkien's epic trilogy, *The Lord of the Rings*, Frodo and Sam are the only characters who complete the entire journey from Hobbiton, a sleepy and comfortable country village, to the rocky and fiery peak of Mount Doom.

Paraphrase

Paraphrases are more detailed than summaries. In a paraphrase, you use your own words to explain the words or sentences of someone else. You should use a paraphrase when a source contains important details or facts that support your main idea.

When you paraphrase, make sure you use original wording and do not change the meaning of the original idea. Paraphrases also require signal phrases and citations.

Here's an example of a paraphrase that uses an MLA-style in-text citation.

Original:	Adolescents can still be persuaded by the messages of advertising, which play into their developmental concerns related to appearance, self-identity, and belonging.
Paraphrase:	Many food advertisements influence adolescents by appealing to common concerns in order to spark an emotional response (Story and French 3).

Quote

To **quote** is to repeat the exact words of a source. Quotations are most effective when the author's language is specific or unique.

When you quote, use quotation marks around the repeated words so that your audience can see the difference between your words and the words of a source.

Quotes always require a citation. In MLA style, this citation comes immediately after the quote. If possible, also use a signal phrase to identify the original author.

Here's an example of a quote with a signal phrase and an in-text citation.

Original:	To Magdalene, problems are tied to places, so traveling is the perfect excuse to escape to a new location and liberate herself from her problems.
Quote:	The article points out that Magdalene's restlessness is caused by her belief that "problems are tied to places" (Pascoe 67).

Chapter 17

MLA

An MLA paper follows a set of standards established by the Modern Language Association for formatting documents and citing sources. When you use MLA style, it allows readers to easily identify important information in your text and even use your work in their own research. MLA style is typically used in the field of humanities, which includes subjects like language, literature, music, history, and anthropology.

17a Formatting the Document

There are specific guidelines for formatting every part of a paper in MLA style:

- Margins, text, and page numbers
- Headings and titles
- Tables and visuals

Margins, Text, and Page Numbers

Margins

The margins should be set at 1 inch on all sides of a standard, 8.5 x 11-inch piece of paper.

To check the margin settings in Microsoft Word, go to the Page Layout tab and click on Margins.

In Pages for Mac, go to the Document tab and click on Document Margins.

Text

Most instructors prefer an easy-to-read font like Times New Roman with a size of 12 points.

Remember to indent the first line of every paragraph by ½ inches. You can usually use the Tab key to do this.

The main text of your paper should be left-aligned. All text, including the works cited and quotations, should be double-spaced.

Generally, MLA style uses the Oxford comma. This means that in a list, a comma is placed in front of the second-to-last item.

> Late musician David Bowie played the keyboard, harmonica, viola, and saxophone, as well as several other instruments.

Only insert one space after a period at the end of a sentence.

Page Numbers

Every page of the MLA document should be numbered.

In the top right-hand corner of each page, type your last name and then the page number.

> Johnson 1

In most word processors, the page number goes in the "Header" and is filled in automatically after you enter the information for the first page.

In Microsoft Word, go to the Insert tab, then Header, and choose the basic, right-aligned option. Alternatively, double-click the top of the page to type directly in the header.

In Pages for Mac, click on the top of the page and type in the header area. Use the toolbar to right-align the text.

Headings and Titles

Heading

MLA research papers do not use title pages unless your instructor asks for one. However, there is a specific MLA heading.

At the top of the first page of your paper, type your name. On the next line, type your instructor's name. Underneath your instructor's name, type the course name. Finally, underneath the course name, enter the date as day-month-year format.

Usually, this is the date that the assignment is due. All of this information should be double-spaced.

Jordan Smith

Professor Johnson

History 102

4 November 2017

Title

One double-spaced line below the heading, write the title of your text. It should be center-aligned. There should also be one double-spaced line between the title and the first paragraph of the paper.

The title doesn't need to be italicized, underlined, or in quotation marks. However, if your title contains the name of an outside source, format the source's title normally.

Humor and Suffering in *The Cherokee Word for Water*

Capitalize the first and last word of a title no matter what. The other words in a title are usually capitalized. However, do not capitalize the following types of words if they come between the first and last word of the title:

- Articles (*a, an, the*)
- Prepositions
- Coordinating conjunctions (FANBOYS)

Tables and Visuals

Tables

Tables should be placed as closely as possible to the section of the paper they relate to.

Label the table as "Table," followed by the number. For example, the second table in an MLA paper would be labeled "Table 2." The label should be left-aligned.

Title the table using the same capitalization rules for other titles. The title should be below the label and left-aligned.

Include the table source, if relevant, as a caption below it. If you would like to include notes on the table, set them apart from regular text by indenting them and using a lowercase letter. All text should be double-spaced.

> Source: Table source

> a. Table notes

Visuals

Photographs, charts, maps, and other visuals are labeled "Fig.," (an abbreviation of *Figure*), numbered, and captioned.

> Fig. 3. Andy Warhol, *Diamond Dust Shoes*, The Andy Warhol Museum, Pittsburg.

The label and caption should be placed below the visual and do not need to be indented.

Musical illustrations, such as sheet music, are labeled "Ex.," (an abbreviation of *Example*), numbered, and captioned.

> Ex. 1. George Gershwin, *Rhapsody in Blue*.

The label and caption should be placed below the musical illustration and do not need to be indented.

17b Citing the Document Sources

Whenever you integrate borrowed ideas or words into your writing, you must credit, or cite, the original source. An MLA paper includes a formal list of Works Cited on the final page(s) of the document. For each entry in the works-cited list, there should be at least one corresponding in-text citation that indicates the borrowed information within the body of the essay. There are specific rules and requirements for utilizing and formatting both in-text citations and entries in a works-cited page.

In-Text Citations

Basic Format

In-text citations appear in parentheses within the body of your paper immediately after summarized, paraphrased, or quoted text. MLA in-text citations generally use an "author-page" format: the author's last name is followed by the page number of the text.

> In the north Atlantic, the life cycles of polar bears and harp seals are inextricably connected (Sanderson 45).

The in-text citation indicates that this idea comes from page forty-five of a work by an author whose last name is Sanderson. Using this information, readers can refer to the works-cited list for more source information.

In-text citations always appear at the end of a sentence, not in the middle.

Incorrect:	Ginny and Lamar are "painfully realistic" (Murray 12) characters; every aspect of their lives is exposed to the reader.
Correct:	Ginny and Lamar are "painfully realistic" characters; every aspect of their lives is exposed to the reader (Murray 12).

Periods, question marks, and exclamation points go *after* an in-text citation, while quotation marks go *before* the in-text citation.

Incorrect:	The bloody, merciless gladiatorial matches of the Roman Empire were entertainment for "spectators that were perhaps even more desensitized to violence than 21st century audiences (Ferelli 139)."
Correct:	The bloody, merciless gladiatorial matches of the Roman Empire were entertainment for "spectators that were perhaps even more desensitized to violence than 21st century audiences" (Ferelli 139).

If the author's name is mentioned in the text itself, only a page number is necessary for the in-text citation.

> In a controversial essay, Lau claims that the American Revolution was not, in fact, a revolution (83).

If you are using more than one source by the same author in your paper, include a shortened version of the source title in the in-text citation.

> In a controversial essay, Lau claims that the American Revolution was not, in fact, a revolution ("American" 83). However, Lau does believe the French Revolution was a true revolution ("Revolutions" 45).

If you cite the same author and work multiple times in a row, only use the author's last name in the first in-text citation. Afterwards, only use the page number until you cite another source.

Citing a Work with Multiple Authors

In an in-text citation of a work with multiple authors, include the last names separated by *and* as well as commas (for more than two authors).

> Overall, people are much more likely to commit objectionable acts if they "believe they are obeying an authority figure" (Smith and Rowe 95).

Citing a Work with No Author

If the author of a source is unknown, include the page number of the quote/summary/paraphrase and an abbreviated version of the source title in quotation marks.

Full Source Title: "1940s Fashion in America"

In-Text Citation: ("1940s Fashion" 12)

Citing a Whole Work

To cite an entire work, like a website or movie, use the title of the source or the name of the author/editor/director in the sentence itself instead of in a parenthetical citation. The information you provide should match the first piece of information in the Works Cited entry.

> Alfred Hitchcock's *Psycho* has influenced nearly every horror movie and thriller that has been produced since then.

> According to Dictionary.com, one definition of "passive" is, "not reacting visibly to something that might be expected to produce manifestations of an emotion or feeling."

Formatting Quotes

Quotations are a powerful tool in a research paper. However, it's not a good strategy to include long passages just to fill up space or to use quotes without introducing or explaining them.

There are a variety of ways you can incorporate quotes in your paper to strengthen your own writing. Formatting these quotes with consistent MLA style will make your paper easy to read and understand.

Prose

"Prose" is how people normally write and speak; newspaper articles, books, and emails are all examples of prose.

If a quote, when typed in your document, is four lines or fewer, it can go directly in the text of your paper. Remember to use quotation marks and an in-text citation.

> When asked for her opinion on private information on the internet, she said, "I call it information inflation. Personal information has all but lost its value because there is so much of it circulating" (Butler 3).

Quotes can be whole sentences, a phrase, or just a few words.

Sentence:	"The low-roofed tavern was like a used-up match: dark and smoky" (Rasha 34).
Phrase:	The author compares the tavern to "a used-up match: dark and smoky" (Rasha 34).

Words: The tavern is described as "smoky" and "low-
roofed" (Rasha 34).

If a quote, when typed in your document, is more than four
lines, it should be separated from the rest of the text in a **block
quote**. Left-align the entire quotation and indent by one inch.
Block quotes should also be double-spaced like the rest of your
paper. Quotation marks aren't necessary, but use an in-text
citation.

> The narrator often engages in conversations with strangers,
> although it's likely that these interactions exist only in the
> speaker's mind.

> > I had a real nice talk with a lady who was
> > sitting on my windowsill. I was just sitting
> > on the floor when I looked up and saw
> > her sitting there like a blue jay. She had
> > just finished working in her garden, and
> > she offered me some green tomatoes and
> > regular tomatoes and lettuce and carrots.
> > I told her I don't much like vegetables, but
> > if she ever took to making jam, she should
> > let me know. There's nothing better in this
> > world than homemade blackberry jam.
> > (Benson 112).

Even if your block quote contains multiple paragraphs, do not
indent the first line of each paragraph.

Poetry

If you quote three lines or fewer of a poem, use quotation
marks and put them directly in the text of your paper. Insert
two forward slashes between each line.

Original:

When the stars threw down their spears

And water'd heaven with their tears:

Did he smile his work to see?

Did he who made the Lamb make thee? (Blake 17-20)

Quoted:

In "The Tyger," William Blake uses repeated questioning to move the poem forward: "Did he smile his work to see? // Did he who made the Lamb make thee" (19-20)?

Instead of using page numbers in the in-text citation, use the range of line numbers of the poem. The example above quotes lines 19 and 20. Most poems indicate line number in increments of five or ten by including small numbers in the left margin of a poem. For the in-text citation, include the numbers only; there's no need to write "lines"

If you quote more than three lines of poetry, set them off from the rest of your paper. Left-align and indent by one inch. Do not use quotation marks, but include the line numbers in an in-text citation.

In Rudyard Kipling's "The Way Through the Woods," the speaker repeats the phrase "road through the woods" as if wearing a path in the reader's mind.

> They shut the road through the woods
>
> Seventy years ago.
>
> Weather and rain have undone it again,
>
> And now you would never know
>
> There was once a road through the woods. (1-5)

After using the basic MLA formatting style, re-format the poem closely as possible to how it appears in the source. Some poems have unconventional spacing.

If the quote begins in the middle of a line, do not align it to the left. Leave it where it is in the original. Here's an example from *Sonnet 116* by William Shakespeare.

Original:

Let me not to the marriage of true minds

Admit impediments. Love is not love

Which alters when it alteration finds,

Or bends with the remover to remove. (1-4)

Quoted:

Shakespeare claims that true love is unchanging:

Love is not love

Which alters when it alteration finds,

Or bends with the remover to remove. (2-4)

Drama

In-text citations for plays include the act, scene, and line number, as well as the abbreviated title. Separate each number with a period. Not all plays are divided into acts or scenes; if so, use as much of the relevant information as possible.

If you quote one character in a play, place it directly in the text of your paper. Here's an example that uses a quote from *Long Day's Journey into Night* by Eugene O'Neill.

Mary expresses her discontentment to her son, saying, "I've never felt it was my home. It was wrong from the start" (*Long* 1).

The in-text citation indicates that this quotation comes from Act 1. This play has no scenes or line numbers, so only the act number is provided.

If you quote dialogue between multiple characters in a play, set it off from the rest of your paper. Left-align and indent by one inch.

Begin each line of dialogue with the character's name in all capital letters, followed by a period. It's not necessary to use quotation marks. After the first line, indent each character's lines by an extra quarter inch. Here's an example that uses dialogue from *Twelfth Night* by William Shakespeare.

> Malvolio, not knowing the letter was written as a prank by Maria, follows its instructions completely.
>
>> MARIA. He's coming madam; but in a very strange manner. He is sure, possessed, madam.
>>
>> OLIVIA. Why, what's the matter? does he rave?
>>
>> MARIA. No, madam, he does nothing but smile: your ladyship were best to have some guard about you, if he come; for sure, the man is tainted in's wits. (*Twelfth* 3.4)

Include stage directions as they appear in the original source or replace them with an ellipsis.

>> MARY [*forcing a smile*]. I have? Nonsense, dear. It's your imagination. [*with sudden tenseness*] You really must not watch me all the time, James. I mean, it makes me self-conscious. (*Long* 1)

Changing Quotes

In general, quotes should be written exactly as they appear in the original. However, sometimes it's necessary to make changes. These changes must be clearly indicated.

If a quote contains an error committed by the original speaker or author, place "(sic)" after it in your paper. *Sic* comes from the Latin word for *thus*.

> He said, "My parents loved to repeat stories about watching the moon landing on TV in 1967 (sic), but I didn't appreciate it at the time."

This quote contains an error because the moon landing happened in 1969, not 1967, so *sic* is placed in parentheses after the error.

If you want to emphasize certain words or phrases in a quote, italicize them and place "(emphasis added)" at the end of the quote.

> Thomas Paine claimed, "Character is much easier *kept* than *recovered*" (emphasis added).

To add explanation or missing words to a quote, use brackets.

> Sir Thomas Wyatt may have been referring to Anne Boleyn in his poem "Whoso List [Wants] to Hunt."

> Tromer was inspired to write by "the lonely masses [of people] passing by the door."

The Works-Cited List

The works-cited section of an MLA paper includes an expanded and organized list of all the sources you cited within the body of your paper.

Formatting the Works-Cited Page

Here are some key rules for proper formatting of a works-cited page:

- The works-cited page should include a header on its top right corner indicating your last name and the page number.
- Enter the title, "Works Cited," on the first line of the page. It should be centered and one inch from the top of the page.
- Double-space between the title and the first entry in your list.
- Double-space and left-align the text within in each line of an entry.

The first line of every entry should be left-aligned and should not include indentations. If an entry exceeds one line, subsequent lines should be indented by 1/2 inch. This is called a **hanging indentation**.

Tomeil, Harrison. "Jesters and Judges in Medieval Legends." *The Journal of Medieval English Studies* vol. 23 (2012): pp. 5-9. *Project Muse.* www.muse.jhu.edu/article/6384.

Organizing the Works-Cited Page

The entries in a works-cited list are arranged alphabetically by the source author's last name. So an entry for "Rowling, J.K." would be listed *after* an entry for "Green, John."

If two authors have the same last name, alphabetize by the first letter of their first name.

Farley, Andrew

Farley, Terri

Farley, Walter

If two or more entries have the same coauthor, alphabetize by the last name of the *second* author listed.

Bakshi, Malia, and Edward Hess

Bakshi, Malia, and Alice Moran

Bakshi, Malia, Logan Zimmer, and Stephen Brown

If an entry has no author, alphabetize by the title. Include any articles (*a, an, the*) as part of the title. For example, *The Encyclopedia of North American Owls* would be alphabetized by the letter *T*.

If a source title begins with a number, alphabetize it as if the number were written out. For example, *1984* (by George Orwell) would be alphabetized by the letter *N* as in *nineteen*.

If your paper cites multiple works by one author, only provide the author's name in the first entry of the works cited list. For the subsequent works, replace the author's name with three hyphens and a period. If the author is also a coauthor, repeat the full name.

Perry, Georgia. "Speech Acts and Childhood Development." Oxford University Press, USA, 2008, New York.

---. "American Linguistics." Simon & Schuster, 2013, New York.

---. "Decoding English Morphemes." Simon & Schuster, 2012, New York.

Perry, Georgia and Ken Bryant. "Borrowing Status: Regional Accents and Prejudice." *Journal of Language* vol. 112 (2014): pp. 89-93. *JSTOR*. www.jstor.org/stable/df.0545.

Source Information in a Works-Cited Entry

Basic Format

Generally, works-cited entries follow this structure:

[Author Name]. [Title of Source]. [Title of Container], [Other Contributors], [Version], [Number], [Publisher], [Publication Date], [Location].

If a source has an editor, compiler, or translator, write out these terms in full.

Here are some examples of works-cited entries:

A Book

Doerr, Anthony. *All the Light We Cannot See*. Scribner, 2014, New York.

Pratchett, Terry. *Going Postal*. HarperCollins Publishers, 2014, New York.

A book's publication information is usually listed in the first few pages. Older books may not have a publisher listed; if that's the case, just include the city and year of publication.

A Book with Two or More Authors

Hutchens, Joy, and Nicole Muniz. *The Blind Window*. East Coast Publishers, 1993, New York.

Notice that a comma comes between the authors' names, and the second author's name is formatted normally: first name, then last name.

A Book with More Than Three Authors

If a printed work has more than three authors, name only the first and then write *et al.*, which is Latin for "and others."

> Dragoumis, Faith, et al. *A Brief History of Mykonos*. JI Press, 1967, Chicago.

A Work from an Anthology

An anthology is a compilation of works or excerpts that are unified by a particular theme. To cite a work included in an anthology, use the following template:

> Marvell, Andrew. "To His Coy Mistress." *Seventeenth Century English Poets*. Michael Hayes, editor. Quill and Ink, 2002, New York, pp. 46-47.

Notice that the citation includes the page range of the entire work within the anthology. Even if you only cite one part of the work, still include the full page range.

An Anthology

To cite an entire anthology, follow this template:

> Isabel, Ortiz, editor. *Peruvian Poets of the 20th Century*. JI Press, 2015, New York.

A Graphic Novel

> Clowes, Daniel. *Patience*. Fantagraphics Books, 2016, Seattle.

If the graphic novel has more than one creator, begin the citation with the name most relevant to your research, along with a label that identifies their role. Later in the entry, list the other creators and their role labels. These labels are often on the graphic novel's cover or title page.

> Lee, Samuel, artist. *Night Owl*. Macey Rowland, writer. Hill Comics, 2015, Chicago.

Articles in Scholarly Journals

A scholarly article is probably one of the most common sources in research papers. Take a look at these examples:

Reed, Andrew. "Career Fixation in America." *Journal of American History,* vol. 108, no. 3, 2011, pp. 45-57.

Massoni, Elizabeth. "Write is Might: Satire and Political Influence in Seventeenth Century England." *Restoration-Era English Literature,* vol. 25, no. 6, 2005, pp. 105-112.

Unavailable Source Information

If parts of this information are unavailable, simply exclude that information from the entry.

Chapter 17 MLA

17c MLA Sample

The header with the author's last name and page number.

Katelynn Ingle

Professor Roberts

ENGL 432

3 November 2014

A double-spaced MLA style heading with the student's name, instructor's name, the course, and the date.

In Our Hands: Responsibility, Gender, and the Holocaust in

Young Adult Fiction

The title of the essay, centered.

    In My Hands is the memoir of Irene Opdyke, a young Polish woman who witnesses and experiences great cruelty during World War II, yet develops compassion and strength. Woven throughout the story of her extraordinary life are issues with which many young adults grapple, like agency, purpose, and responsibility. *In My Hands* is an excellent addition to a syllabus for young adult literature course for several reasons. In simple but beautiful language, it combines history and personal memory to create a unique yet familiar perspective. Additionally, it consciously and appropriately engages the topic of the Holocaust in four primary ways to explore its historical implications and provoke vital questions about the nature of evil and personal responsibility.

    In "A New Algorithm of Evil," Elizabeth Baer discusses how to select books about the Holocaust. Though Baer's article primarily addresses how to identify the "usefulness and effectiveness" of Holocaust literature for children, the principles are the same for readers of all ages (384). She proposes four criteria for addressing broader and more philosophical issues in Holocaust narratives. The first condition is that these books "must grapple directly with the evil of the Holocaust" (383). People often state, correctly, that the Holocaust and its evil must be remembered in order to prevent it from recurring. However, Baer points out that most young readers are learning about the Holocaust for the first time, "and indeed, as more time elapses between the Holocaust and the present, this will be true of all readers" (380). *In My Hands* is not gratuitous in its depiction of the horrors of World War II, but it also does not omit or sidestep it. Opdyke describes how she and her family endured occupation by the Nazis, who despised Polish people. They were dislocated from their homes, separated from their families, and forced to work for the Nazis. Their food was rationed severely, and they were under constant threat of physical harm or even death. Irene

Since the sentence references the author's last name, "Baer," only the page number is necessary for the in-text citation.

Ingle 2

discovers that the Jews are experiencing persecution on an even larger scale and to a more extreme extent. While she is visiting friends in a Jewish ghetto, Nazis raid the houses and take many of the residents to labor camps. Irene herself grapples with the evil she witnesses. As she hides in an abandoned home, she watches an officer throw into the air and shoot what at first appears to be a bird, until she realizes "it was not a bird," but a child (Opdyke and Armstrong 117). Several times throughout the book, Opdyke alludes to this tragic scene and the "bird," at first unable to admit what she really saw. However, she eventually allows herself to confront reality. Irene's innocence and gradual exposure parallels the realizations of young adult readers who learn about the evil of the Holocaust.

The second criterion that Baer suggests is that a Holocaust narrative should not be over-simplified; instead it should ask "difficult questions for which there are no formulaic answers" (384). Opdyke's narrative captures this complexity, particularly as she forms relationships. After she is beaten and assaulted by Russian soldiers, she is take under the wing of a kindly Russian doctor, Dr. Olga Pavlovskaya. Later, she works under Herr Schulz, a German cook who feeds and cares for Irene and her sister. Eventually, when Irene begins undermining the Nazis and sheltering Jews, he looks the other way. However, she struggles to resolve his kindness with the cruelty of every other German she has encountered: "he made hating the Germans a complex matter, when it should have been such a straight-forward one" (Opdyke and Armstrong 134). Opdyke's recollections of cruelty and kindness from people who should have been her enemies are thought-provoking for readers because they don't allow simple and stark categorization.

Baer's third criterion is broad, and probably one of the most obvious things that is to be expected in this genre of literature, but nonetheless important: Holocaust narratives must strongly caution against "racism," "anti-Semitism," and "complacency" (385). Baer does not elaborate any further on this point, but it is the baseline requirement that an educator, parent, or publisher should consider when evaluating a book about the Holocaust. Opdyke recounts her confusion as to why the Nazis specifically targeted the Jews: "It had never occurred to me to distinguish between people based on their religion" (Opdyke and Armstrong 18). Her statements apply to the senseless nature, not just of anti-Semitism, but prejudice in general. Poland, with its own rich culture and history, was reduced by the Nazis to "a land of Slavic brutes, fit only for labor" (18). Irene's narrative demonstrates the ripple effect of prejudice, racism, and genocide. It raises questions for young readers about where the stopping point is if cruelty is allowable based only on what makes one person different from another.

Since this is the first quotation from this source, in the in-text citation includes the authors' names as well as the page number.

In My Hands is also uniquely suited to Baer's fourth consideration for Holocaust literature because it encourages "a sense of personal responsibility" (385). Opdyke's first-person narrative draws the reader into her perspective as she develops her own sense of responsibility for the Jews' suffering. At first, she feels helpless and swept along by forces greater than herself. But after witnessing the cruelty of the Nazis, she quickly develops a feeling of personal responsibility and empathy for what is happening. When she witnesses Nazis shoot an elderly Jewish man, she "felt a scream rising . . . as though I had been shot myself" (Opdyke and Armstrong 102). This moment is a turning point for Irene; immediately afterwards, she steals food from the hotel kitchen where she works and leaves it outside a Jewish ghetto. Irene's story proves that even a young female in a seemingly helpless position can exert agency and subvert corrupt powers. Louise O. Vasvári writes that this area of literature "still tends to privilege the Holocaust experience of men as universal" (1).

At the beginning of her story, Irene is young and female, and therefore vulnerable both in her own eyes and the eyes of society: "I was only a girl, alone among the enemy. What could I do?" (Opdyke and Armstrong 121). However, as her resistance efforts continue, she takes ownership of her femininity, so that her "weakness" becomes her "advantage" (124). She spies on German officers and passes along information to the ghetto, supports a group of Jewish workers, and eventually hides them in the basement of a Nazi major's villa. Later, she joins a Polish partisan group that sabotages and undermines the Nazis, all the while escaping detection by using gender stereotypes to her advantage. Her reputation as a resistance fighter spreads until she is suspected by the enemy to be the rebels' leader. The phrase "only a girl" echoes throughout her narrative, becoming an ironic mantra as she flouts what her enemies expect of a young female. Opdyke's unique perspective is vital for both male and female young adult readers because she took action instead of complying with cultural and societal expectations.

In My Hands addresses issues facing young adults, like identity, responsibility, and agency while providing a compelling and thought-provoking depiction of the Holocaust. Opdyke's willingness to recount her experiences allows others to grapple with the complexity of evil and personal responsibility. Her personal growth as an adolescent woman and her unique perspective as a female during the occupation of Poland is inspiring to men and women alike. The novel's simple and expressive language makes it an ideal literary, as well as historical and philosophical, addition not just to Holocaust literature, but literature in general.

Ingle   4

Works Cited

Baer, Elizabeth Roberts. "A New Algorithm in Evil: Children's Literature in a Post-Holocaust World." *The Lion and the Unicorn* vol. 24 no. 3, 2000, pp. 378-401.

Opdyke, Irene Gut, and Jennifer Armstrong. *In My Hands: Memories of a Holocaust Rescuer.* Dell Laurel-Leaf, 1999, New York.

Vasvári, Louise O. "Bibliography of Central European Women's Holocaust Life Writing in English." *Library Series, CLCWeb: Comparative Literature and Culture*, 2012, www.docs.lib.purdue.edu/clcweblibrary/vasvariceushoahbib/

The page numbers continue onto the Works Cited page.

The title, "Works Cited," centered at the top of the page.

The works cited entries are in alphabetical order by the authors' last names, starting with B.

The citation for an article in a scholarly journal.

The citation for a printed book.

The works cited entry for an article in a scholarly journal.

Chapter 18

APA

Whether you're at school or working in a professional setting, you may be asked to write in APA style. APA stands for American Psychological Association, and it's most commonly used in the social sciences. In particular, disciplines like anthropology, sociology, economics, psychology, and history use this style guide most often.

18a Formatting the Document

APA requires very specific guidelines when formatting a paper. Below is a list of items with particular conditions:

- General formatting: margins, text, page numbers, and headers
- Title pages
- Abstracts
- The body of the paper
- References
- Footnotes
- Tables and figures
- Appendices

General Formatting

Margins
- The margins should be set at 1 inch on all sides
- Use an 8.5 x 11-inch piece of paper

Text
- Papers should be typed in an easy-to-read font at size 10 or 12
- Double-space the entire paper with two spaces in-between sentences
- Left-align all text

- Indent the first line of every paragraph by ½ inch

Headers and Page Numbers
- APA style headers include the title of your paper and the page number
- Page numbers should start on the title page with the number 1 and be right-aligned
- The title of your paper should be written in capital letters and left-aligned
- Titles are normally twelve words or fewer, with a maximum of 50 characters

Exercise

Below is a list of possible titles of papers. Practice shortening them so that they will fit in an APA style header, with 12 words or fewer and no more than 50 characters.

How Discrimination Can Negatively Impact Children and Adolescences, Ages 7-14, in the United States and Canada

Using Novels in the Classroom and Their Positive Effects on the Classroom Environment and Classroom Management System

Social Media and the Portrayal of Workplace Violence in the Last Three Decades and the Effect on Relationships

The Symptoms of Post-Traumatic Stress Disorder and the Benefits of Hypnosis, Meditation, and Yoga

Title Page

APA style papers require a title page. The title page has five parts:

- running head
- title
- author byline
- affiliation
- author note

Remember that this will be the first page of your paper and should be numbered as page 1.

Running Head

The title page has a different header from the rest of your paper. Before the capitalized title of your paper, include the words "Running head" followed by a colon.

In your word processor, you may need special settings that allow your title page header to be different from the rest of your paper.

Title, Author Byline, and Affiliation

In the upper half of the title page, type the full title of your paper.

Below the title, type the author byline: your first name, middle initial (if applicable), and last name.

If your paper has more than one author (for example, if it's a group project) list the authors in order of their contribution to the paper. For two authors, separate their names with the word *and*.

For more than two authors, separate their names with commas and include the word *and* before the last contributor.

> Kyle B. Edwards and Marissa T. Brown
>
> Whitney Post, Samantha L. Ruiz, and Matthew J. Henson

Below the author byline, type the affiliation of the contributors. Normally, this is the institution, school, or organization that the authors are representing.

All of this text should be center-aligned.

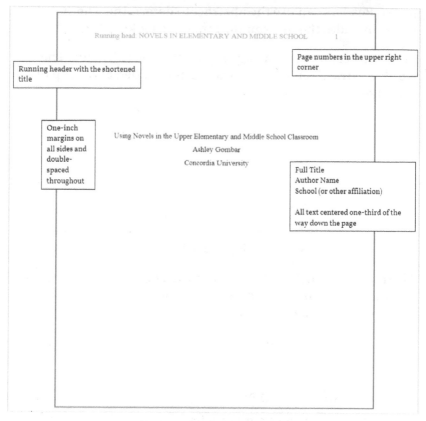

Figure 5.1

Author's Note

Sometimes, the title page also includes an author's note. An author's note can contain specifics on affiliation (including departments or changes to the document), acknowledgments, special circumstances, contact information for readers, and/or disclaimers.

Authors' notes are less frequent in academic writing; they're more common in published papers.

Abstract

If you have ever done research in a scholarly journal, you have probably read an abstract. An **abstract** is a short summary of a paper. Readers can use the abstract to determine whether the paper includes the information they are looking for.

The abstract has its own page right after the title page. The word **"Abstract"** should be centered and bolded at the top of the page.

NOVELS IN ELEMENTARY AND MIDDLE SCHOOL   2

Abstract

This paper will discuss the importance of fiction novels during the formative years of

elementary and middle school (approximately ages 8-13). Because this period of time involves

social, intellectual, and mental development, as well as language acquisition, both parents and

Figure 5.2

Abstracts are usually 150-250 words. It's best to write your abstract *after* writing your paper so that you can be sure to include all the major points.

Insert a page break after the abstract to ensure that it is the only thing on the page.

The Body of the Paper

The body of the paper begins on its own page after the title page and the abstract page. At the top of this page, type the full title of your paper and center-align it. Do not underline, bold, or italicize the title.

Headings

APA style uses headings to separate the different parts of a paper. There are five different levels of headings, though you may not necessarily use all of them.

Level	Alignment	Formatting	Capitalization and Punctuation
Level 1 (title)	Centered	**Bold**	All major words
Level 2	Left-aligned	**Bold**	All major words

Level	Alignment	Formatting	Capitalization and Punctuation
Level 3	Indented from left	**Bold**	Only first word + period
Level 4	Indented from left	***Bold + italicized***	Only first word + period
Level 5	Indented from left	*Italicized*	Only first word + period

Level One Heading

Level Two Heading

Level three heading.

Level four heading.

Level five heading.

Figure 5.3

Sections

APA style papers often discuss a completed study or articles based on a study. When this is the case, your professor may ask that you use traditional APA style sections.

There are four sections:

1. Introduction: this section discusses the question or problem.

   - Why is this topic important?
   - What hypotheses were explored?
   - What is the previous work on the same topic?

2. Method: this section describes how the study was conducted.

   - What types of participants did it conclude?
   - What size was the sample and what length of time did it cover?

- How was the research designed and how did it measure data?

3. Results: in this section, the results from the study are revealed.

- What data was collected?
- What statistics and data analysis were used and what did they uncover?
- What was the baseline data and were there any inventions or adverse events?

4. Discussion: here, you will form your own interpretations, inferences, and conclusions.

- What do the results mean?
- Were the hypotheses disproved?
- What does this study teach us?
- What further work could be done on the subject?

Depending on the purpose of the paper, you can use these section names or create your own. See the essay sample in Section 18c for an example of specific paper headings and sections.

References

This is a list of all the sources that you used in your paper that comes after the paper itself. This list always starts on a new page.

This page has the same header as the rest of the paper. The Level 1 heading, or title, is called References.

The citations on the References page should have a "hanging indent" format. This means that every line of a reference, after the first, is indented.

NOVELS IN ELEMENTARY AND MIDDLE SCHOOL 5

References

Anderson, N.A., & Hite, C.E. (2010). Building comprehension for reading novels: The pre-reading schema building process. *New England Reading Association Journal*, 45(2), 26-31, 102-103.

Archer, L.E. (2010). Lexile reading growth as a function of starting level in at-risk middle school students. *Journal of Adolescent & Adult Literacy*, 54(4), 281-290. doi: 10.1598/JAAL.54.4.6

Brenna, B. (2012). How graphic novels support reading comprehension strategy development in children. *Literacy*, 47(2), 88-94. doi: 10.1111/j.1741-4369.2011.00655.x

Bushman, J.H. (March 1997). Young adult literature in the classroom–or is it? *English Journal*, 86(3), 45-40. doi: 10.2207/820642

Figure 5.4

Footnotes

APA papers use footnotes for two main purposes:

- Extra content information
- Copyright information

The footnotes should be brief. They have their own page and a Level 1 heading: Footnotes.

Footnotes for extra content are used to explain information that does not need to be included in the paper but does provide supplemental details to the audience.

Footnotes for copyright information are included if you have obtained permission to reprint or reproduce a copyrighted work.

Tables & Figures

All tables and figures are added after the footnotes.

Tables

Each table should have its own page and a label, starting with **Table 1** as a Level 1 heading. Under each label, write the full title of the table.

HUMAN EATING PATTERNS   7

Table 1

Average Time Spent Eating Per Day

Participant	Time (hr)	Participant	Time (hr)	Participant	Time (hr)
1001	3.0	1006	0.8	1011	3.1
1002	1.0	1007	2.6	1012	4.0
1003	1.5	1008	0.7	1013	1.1
1004	2.2	1009	1.4	1014	0.5
1005	3.5	1009	2.1	1015	1.4

Figure 5.5

In the text of your paper, you can then refer to the tables by their labels.

> The number of correct responses was tallied for each participant (see Table 2).

Figures

Figures can be graphs, drawings, or photographs listed after tables. Each figure has its own page.

Similar to tables, figures have labels, starting with **Figure 1** as a Level 1 heading, and in the text you can refer to them by their labels.

Appendices

Appendices are used to include extra information that would be distracting within the body of the paper.

Here are some examples of appendices:

> A survey used in an experiment

> A description of a piece of equipment used in an experiment

> Mathematical proofs included in a study

Appendix A

Student Reading Survey

Directions: Please answer the questions honestly; there are no right or wrong answers.

On a scale of 1 (completely disagree) to 5 (completely agree), circle your response to the following statements.

1. Reading is easy for me.

| 1 | 2 | 3 | 4 | 5 |

2. I enjoy reading.

| 1 | 2 | 3 | 4 | 5 |

Figure 5.6

If you only have one item in your appendix, label it **Appendix** as a Level 1 heading. If you have more than one item, each item should be on its own page and labeled **Appendix A, Appendix B**, and so on.

In the text of your paper, you can refer to the appendices by their labels.

Each participant received a questionnaire (see Appendix A) to complete.

Exercise

Below is a list of all the possible components of an APA style paper, in no particular order. Re-order the list by labeling them 1-11.

___Tables	___Footnotes	___Figures
___Discussion	___Appendices	___Abstract
___Method	___Results	___Introduction
___Title Page	___References	

18b Citing the Document Sources

In-Text Citations

In-text citations appear in parentheses within the body of your paper immediately after summarized, paraphrased, or quoted text. APA uses an author-date citation system, which uses the author's last name and the year of the source's publication. In-text citations should correspond with entries on the References page.

There are a few places an in-text citation can appear in a sentence.

The author's name can be mentioned in the sentence, directly followed by the year.

> Lambert (2005) claims that previous studies on human obedience all have the same major flaw.

Both the year and the author's name can be mentioned in the sentence.

> In 2005, Lambert claimed that previous studies on human obedience all have the same major flaw.

Or, both the author/s name and publication year can be included in parentheses at the end of the sentence separated by a comma.

> Previous studies on human obedience all have the same major flaw (Lambert, 2005).

If a source has two authors, the names are always cited together. When the names are included within a sentence, separate them with the word *and*. In parentheses, separate the authors' names with an ampersand.

References Page Entry:

> Ivey, G., & Johnston, P. H. (2013). Engagement with young adult literature: Outcomes and processes. *Reading Research Quarterly*, 48(3), 255. doi: 10.1002/rrq.46

In-Text Citation:

Ivey and Johnston (2013) discuss the relevance of novels within the classroom.

Current novels are more relevant to students because they deal in a time period that is relatable (Ivey & Johnston, 2013).

If a work has three to five authors, list all of the names the first time you cite that source in your paper. After that, only write the first name followed by *et al* (which is Latin for "and others") and the publication year.

References Page Entry:

Shank, G., Brown, L. & Pringle J. (2014). *Understanding education research: A guide to critical reading*. Boulder, CO: Paradigm Publishers.

First In-Text Citation: (Shank, Brown, & Pringle, 2014).

Following In-Text Citations: (Shank, et al., 2014).

If a work has six or more authors, include the first surname, followed by *et al.* and the publication year.

References Page Entry:

Denton, C.A., Enos, M., York, M.J., Francis, D.J., Barnes, M.A., Kulesz, P.A., Fletcher, J.M., & Carter, S. (2015). Text-processing differences in adolescent adequate and poor comprehenders reading accessible and challenging narrative and informational text. *Reading Research Quarterly*. doi:10.1002/rrq.105

Correct: (Denton, et al., 2015)

Incorrect: (Denton, Enos, York, Francis, Barnes, Kulesz, Fletcher, & Carter, 2015)

If a source does not have a specified author, use a few words from the References entry instead, usually from the title of the source.

(*Ethical theories*, 2012)

If you cite two sources in the same sentence, list the citations in the parentheses in the order they are cited in the sentence and separate them with a semicolon.

(Ivey & Johnston, 2013; Brown, 2003).

Formatting Quotes

When directly quoting a source, there are a few things to remember.

Any words taken from a source must be written as they originally were.

Original: The fastest way to people's hearts is through their eyes.

Incorrect: "The quickest way to people's hearts is through the eyes."

Correct: Murray states, "The fastest way to people's hearts is through their eyes."

Include the page numbers of the quoted material. If the source has no page numbers, include paragraph numbers if possible.

Notice the abbreviations for *page*, *pages*, and *paragraph*.

- Page = p.
- Pages = pp.
- Paragraph = para.

Quotes shorter than forty words can be included within your sentences. However, quotes longer than forty words should be treated as **block quotes**. To format a block quote, follow these guidelines:

1. Start the quote on a new line, separate from regular text

2. Indent the text ½ inches from the left

3. Do not use quotation marks

4. Double space the entire quote

5. After the final punctuation mark, include an in-text citation with the author's last name, the source's publication year, and the page number

> The characters, and the concept of freedom, was explained in terms close to apathy.
>
> > They were old enough to be irritable when and where they chose, tired enough to look forward to death, disinterested enough to accept the idea of pain while ignoring the presences of pain. They were, in fact and at last, free. (Morrison, 1970, p. 139)

Exercise

Rewrite the following passage so that the quotation and in-text citation are formatted correctly.

In 1970, Morrison described topics of beauty in a way that hits a cord. . . "Along with the idea of romantic love, she was introduced to another- physical beauty. Probably the most destructive ideas in the history of human thought. Both originated in envy, thrived in insecurity, and ended in disillusion. In equating physical beauty with virtue, she stripped her mind, bound it. And collected self-contempt by the heap." (Toni Morrison, *The Bluest Eye*, pgs. 122, 1970).

Formatting the References

The APA References list is a collection of all the sources you cited in your paper.

Page Formatting

At the top of the page, type **References** as a Level 1 heading.

The References list should begin on a new page. It should also have the same header as the rest of the paper.

Each entry should have a hanging indent. For more information on indentation, see the previous section under "References."

Order

All entries should be alphabetized by the authors' last names.

If you have more than one entry by the same author, put them in order of publication date with the earliest coming first.

Brown, D. (1998). *Digital Fortress*. New York: St. Martin's Press.

Brown, D. (2003). *The Da Vinci Code*. New York: Anchor Books.

If you cite two sources with the same first author, use the next author's name to alphabetize them.

Payne, R. K., DeVol, P.E., & Dreussi Smith, T. (2006). *Bridges out of poverty: Strategies for professionals and communities*. Highlands, TX: Aha! Process.

Payne, R. K. & Slocumb, P.D. (2011). *Boys in poverty: A framework for understanding dropout*. Bloomington, IN: Solution Tree.

If there is no author listed, alphabetize by the first important word in the title; ignore articles: *a*, *an*, and *the*.

Incorrect	Correct
A theoretical practice.	The afterthought of courtesy.
Breaking the mold.	Breaking the mold.
The afterthought of courtesy.	A theoretical practice.

Occasionally, a work may be signed as "Anonymous." If this is the case, use Anonymous as if it were the author's last name.

Entries

The purpose of the References list is to give the reader enough information to locate the sources that you used in your paper. For this reason, APA Reference entries include the information needed to search a library catalog or online database:

- author information
- publication date
- title
- publishing information
- electronic location information (if necessary)

Author Information

Authors' last names should come first, followed by their first and middle initials.

> Brown, D. (2003). *The Da Vinci Code*. New York: Anchor Books.

If you have two authors with the same last name and first initial, write their full first names.

> Brown, Dan (2003). *The Da Vinci Code*. New York: Anchor Books.

> Brown, Dee (1971). *Bury my heart at Wounded Knee: An Indian history of the American west*. New York: Holt, Rinehart & Winston.

Use commas to separate author names; last names and first initials; and initials and suffixes, like "Jr." or "III."

> Shank, G., Brown, L. & Pringle J. (2014). *Understanding education research: A guide to critical reading*. Boulder, CO: Paradigm.

To cite a work with multiple authors, use commas and an ampersand.

McGill-Franzen, A., Allington, R. L., Yokoi, L., & Brooks, G.(1999). Putting books in the classroom seems necessary but not sufficient. *The Journal of Educational Research*, 93(2), 67-69. Retrieved from http://search. proquest.com/docview/204261995?accountid=10248

If the work is authored by a group or organization, spell out the full name.

Grolier Incorporated. (2004). *Grolier Student Encyclopedia*.

Danbury, CT: Author.

If a work has no author listed, move the title to the author's name position before the publication date.

Ethical theories [pdf]. (n.d.). Retrieved from http://cup. blackboard.com bbcswebdav/pid-610431- dt-content-rid-17874914_1/courses/20152023543/resources/week2/ethicalTheories.pdf

Publication Date

The year the work was published should be given in parentheses followed by a period.

Shank, G., Brown, L. & Pringle J. (2014). *Understanding education research: A guide to critical reading*. Boulder, CO: Paradigm.

For **periodical** works that are published multiple times on exact dates—like magazines, newsletters and newspapers—provide the year and as much of the date as possible in parentheses.

Moore, L. (2016, March 31). Running in Cuba. *New York Times*. Retrieved from http://well.blogs.nytimes. com/2016/03/31/running-in-cuba/?ref=health

If no date is provided, write "n.d." in parentheses.

Beckerman, C.D., Heavenridge, P. & Shelton L. (n.d.). Multiple intelligences for adult literacy and education: *Assessment: find your strengths*. Retrieved from http://

www.literacynet.org/mi/assessment/findyourstrengths.
html

Title

Formatting a source's title depends on the type of work.

Books and Reports
- Only capitalize the first letter of the title, any proper nouns, and the first letter of the subtitle (if relevant)

- Italicize the title

- End with a period

Brown, D. (2003). *The Da Vinci code.* New York: Anchor Books.

Periodical Sources (journals, newsletters, and magazines)
- Capitalize all of the important words in the title

- Italicize the title

- End with a period if the source is electronic

- End with a comma if the source is print

Moore, L. (2016, March 31). Running in Cuba. *New York Times.* Retrieved from http://well.blogs.nytimes.com/2016/03/31/running-in-cuba/?ref=health

Articles and Chapters Within a Book, Journal, or Magazine
- Only capitalize the first letter of the title, any proper nouns, and the first letter of the subtitle (if relevant)

- Do not italicize, underline, or use quotation marks

- End with a period

McGill-Franzen, A., Allington, R. L., Yokoi, L., & Brooks, G. (1999). Putting books in the classroom seems necessary but not sufficient. *The Journal of Educational Research,* 93(2), 67. Retrieved from http://search.proquest.com/docview/204261995?accountid=10248

There may be times when it is important to include extra information with the title in order for your reader to effectively locate your sources. If so, use brackets to add the information after the title.

Here are some examples of extra information:

[Abstract]   [Special issue]

[Motion Picture]   [Audio podcast]

[CD]   [Brochure]

[Letter to the editor]

Publication Information

Depending on the type of work you are citing, the publication information will vary.

Books and Reports
- Provide the location of publication, followed by a colon
- City and state if in the U.S.
- City and country if outside of the U.S.
- Provide the name of the publishing company, followed by a period.
- Capitalize
- Do not include "Publishers," "Co.," or "Inc."
- If the author is the publisher, use "Author" to indicate publisher

Brown, D. (2003). *The Da Vinci code*. New York: Anchor Books.

Grolier Incorporated. (2004). *Grolier Student Encyclopedia*. Danbury, CT: Author.

Periodical Sources (journals, newsletters, and magazines)
- Provide volume number and italicize it
- If the issue number is provided, include it in parentheses, followed by a comma
- Give page or page range used in the paper, followed by a period

Ivey, G., & Johnston, P. H. (2013). Engagement with young adult literature: Outcomes and processes. *Reading Research Quarterly, 48*(3), 255. doi: 10.1002/rrq.46

McGill-Franzen, A., Allington, R. L., Yokoi, L., & Brooks, G. (1999). Putting books in the classroom seems necessary but not sufficient. *The Journal of Educational Research, 93*(2), 67-69. Retrieved from http://search.proquest.com/docview/204261995?accountid=10248

Electronic Location Information

Now that so much information can be found online, it's important to include enough information for internet sources to help your readers.

Online sources should include as much regular information as possible. Some sources may have all of these parts, while others may only have one or two.

- author information
- publication date
- title
- publishing information

After these elements, include the electronic location information. A URL is the unique web address of every page on the internet. If your source is online, include the URL. At the end of the reference entry, type "Retrieved from" and include the complete URL.

McGill-Franzen, A., Allington, R. L., Yokoi, L., & Brooks, G. (1999). Putting books in the classroom seems necessary but not sufficient. *The Journal of Educational Research, 93*(2), 67. Retrieved from http://search.proquest.com/docview/204261995?accountid=10248

18c APA Sample

The following example essay follows the APA Guidelines.

Quality Education for Students of Poverty   1

The Running head includes the title shortened to no more than 50 characters. It is labeled as a "Running head" only on the Title Page.

Quality Education for Students of Poverty

Training Teachers to Even the Playing Field

Ashley Mclauchlan

Caldwell University

Full title, author name, and institution are placed one-third of the way down the Title Page.

Author's Note indicates more specific information about the paper.

Author Note

This report was presented to Helen Smith of Caldwell University for the fulfillment of Online

English Courses.

Page numbers are placed on the top right-hand side of each page.

Abstract

This paper explores the negative impacts of poverty on student learning and strategies that schools can implement for tackling those challenges. Teachers must find literature that students, no matter what socioeconomic status, can relate to and learn from. This ability in teachers comes from quality training, abundant resources, and solid relationships with students.

If included, the Abstract summarizes the topic of the paper.

The full title is centered on the first line(s) of the first page of the body text.

Quality Education for Students of Poverty:
Training Teachers to Even the Playing Field

      Many aspects of the classroom contribute to the learning that takes place there. Taking into account the different cultures, socioeconomic status (SES) characteristics, family layouts, multiple intelligences, and teacher training is vital to success. Providing literature to a classroom of students is also vital to their success, but the presence of these resources is not enough.

Literacy Struggle

Level One Heading

      As stated in the Bushman (1997) article, educators need to choose the literature they expose to their students carefully in order to inspire continued reading, but this presentation of literature is a learned skill. Many educators admit that the literacy struggle with students begins because text is not a part of their everyday lives. Homes of under-privileged children often do not have books readily available or provide modeling of regular and consistent reading for pleasure or learning. These issues are evident in early grades, but are habits that affect students throughout their education.

Level Two Heading

The Role of Poverty

      One of the biggest obstacles for students is rooted in poverty. Payne (1996) outlined the difference between the middle class frame of mind and the driving forces in the lives of those living in poverty. These "hidden rules" are evident drastically within the classroom. Payne (1996) outlined clearly by stating, "Quite simply, one rule is that non-verbal communication is much more important than verbal communication. A second rule is that physical fighting is often necessary for survival" when describing the actions of a child in poverty (p. 1). These differences need to be noticed by teachers in order to understand the actions and thoughts of students and provide relevant learning.

Direct quotes require page number at the end of the sentence because date and author were included within the text.

A Study of the Benefits of Teacher Training

      The training of teachers is vital to the effective teaching of literature, demonstrated by McGill-Frazen, Allington, Yokum, & Brooks (1999) in their study of six full-day kindergarten classes in a large urban school district (p. 68). Three different groups were formed in order to collect data. The first was a controlled classroom where no books were added, and no training

The first occurrence of this in-text citation contains all author names.

was conducted. The second was a books-only classroom where 250 children's books were given to the classroom and parents had a library of books, but no training was conducted. The third group consisted of classrooms with 250 books, a parent library, and a total of 30 hours of training for each teacher (McGill-Frazen, et al, 1999, p. 68). A number of standardized assessments collected data from 377 students as both pretests and posttests, observations were made of the learning environments, and teacher logs were collected (McGill-Frazen, et al, 1999, p. 69).

All author names are not needed here because it is the second in-text citation for this source.

Results

The findings made it clear how important it is to provide teacher training along with resources. Often, schools think that giving the correct resources to teachers will solve problems, but that is clearly not the case.

Discussion

Level Two Heading

Professional development needs to focus on using the resources provided to ensure resources benefit the growth of students. It is unfortunate that no information was given about how the books added to these classrooms were chosen, the details about the training provided to teachers, and/or any data collected concerning the parent lending library and if this lending library inspired any literacy exposure at home. These points would have been interesting insights into the introduction of literature into the classroom. Also, it would have been interesting to have students and parents complete a survey (for example see Appendix A), to collect data on their thoughts towards literature.

Extra information can be provided in appendices.

Though this study was conducted with kindergarten teachers, it is clear that the findings would apply to literature and training in all grades; teachers cannot just read novels with students, they must truly engage and teach literacy skills with rich text. Getting a class set of novels is not going to transform the learning environment, reading abilities, or attitudes towards reading in a classroom, but pair quality literature with a trained, effective teacher, and the possibilities are endless.

List of References
should be on its
own page Title
is bolded and
centered- level one
heading

Month is included
(no day was
included in this
article) because it is
a periodical

Doi is included
when possible.

URL included in doi
is not available.

References

Bushman, J.H. (March 1997). Young adult literature in the classroom- or is it? *English Journal,*
        86(3), 35-40. doi: 10.2307/820642

McGill-Franzen, A., Allington, R. L., Yokoi, L., & Brooks, G. (1999). Putting books in the class-
        room seems necessary but not sufficient. *The Journal of Educational Research,* 93(2),
        67-69. doi: 10.1080/00220679909597631

Payne, R. (1996). Understanding and working with students and adults from poverty. *Instruction-*
        al Leadership IX(2). Retrieved from http://homepages.wmich.edu/~ljohnson/Payne.pdf

Appendix A

Student Reading Survey

Directions: Please answer the questions honestly; there are no right or wrong answers.

On a scale of 1 (not really my thing) to 5 (expert status) rate yourself in these categories.

1. How would you rate yourself as a reader?

   1   2   3   4   5   6   7   8   9   10

2. How much do you enjoy reading?

   1   2   3   4   5   6   7   8   9   10

3. How well do you understand what you read?

   1   2   3   4   5   6   7   8   9   10

4. How well do you sound out new words?

   1   2   3   4   5   6   7   8   9   10

5. How well do you figure out definitions of unknown words?

   1   2   3   4   5   6   7   8   9   10

Please write your answers to the following questions. Be as descriptive as possible.

6. What are your strengths as a reader?

7. What are your weaknesses as a reader?

8. What is the best book you have ever read?

9. If you could choose to read about anything, what would your choice be?

10. Do you ever read outside of school? If so, how much? If no, why not?

*Appendices
are labeled
A, B, C etc.*

Chapter 19

CMS

The *Chicago Manual of Style* is a style guide created by the University of Chicago Press. It is one of the oldest and most comprehensive style guides available, and is now in its 16th edition. *The Chicago Manual of Style,* often referred to as simply "Chicago," is used primarily for literature and the arts. Because authors, editors, and book publishers utilize this style guide the most, it has been called "the editor's bible."

19a Formatting the Document

There are two main guidelines to consider for formatting a paper in CMS style:

- Margins and alignment
- Creating a title page

Margins and Alignment

There are often specific stipulations for setting up a paper with different formatting standards. When setting up a paper in CMS, follow the guidelines below:

- Page Size: 8.5" x 11"
- Page Margins: 1" on all sides
- Font: 12-point Times New Roman or Palatino
- Alignment: Left
- Spacing: Double

Title Page

Writing an essay in CMS requires a title page. This page has several parts.

The most obvious is the title itself, located a third of the way down the page. If your paper has a subtitle, it belongs on the line below the title, and the title should end in a colon.

Next is the author's name and any other pertinent information (such as the class and instructor). This should be a few lines below the title.

All of the text on the title page should be aligned to the center. Additionally, this page should not have a header or page numbers, though the rest of the essay should.

Getting to Know Billy the Kid:

An in-depth look at the famous outlaw

Jenni Tyler

Folklore 101, Professor Fredrickson

19b Citing the Document Sources

CMS has two distinct ways of documenting sources using citations: the first is the notes and bibliography system, and the second is the author-date system. Each system is preferred by different academic groups, so deciding which to use may depend on what discipline you are working within.

Notes and Bibliography (NB)

The NB system is used primarily in the arts and humanities. In the NB system, writers reference sources using footnotes. A **footnote** is a note in a paragraph that tells the reader which words and ideas come from a source. The footnote corresponds to an entry in the **bibliography**, the list of sources at the end of a text. Let's take a look at an example:

> Fred Harvey's restaurants provided opportunity to women like they had never seen. The chain of southwest restaurants is credited to Fred Harvey, who immigrated to America in 1850. He learned about the restaurant world working as a busboy in New York.[2] Fred Harvey had an entrepreneurial spirit and creative genius that saw an opportunity where none had been before. Having experienced terrible dining options while traveling by train, Harvey knew something had to change, and he was just the man to change it.

> 2. Rosa Walston Latimer, *Harvey Houses of New Mexico: Historic Hospitality from Raton to Deming* (Arcadia Publishing & The History Press, 2015), 12 – 25.

Author-Date (AD)

The AD system is primarily used in the sciences and social sciences. In the AD system, names, dates, and page numbers are included in parentheses in the text and correspond to an entry in the bibliography. Let's take a look at an example:

> Fred Harvey's restaurants provided opportunity to women like they had never seen. The chain of southwest restaurants is credited to Fred Harvey, who immigrated to America in 1850. He learned about the restaurant world

working as a busboy in New York (Latimer 2015, 12–13). Fred Harvey had an entrepreneurial spirit and creative genius that saw an opportunity where none had been before. Having experienced terrible dining options while traveling by train, Harvey knew something had to change, and he was just the man to change it.

Walston Latimer, Rosa. 2015. *Harvey Houses of New Mexico: Historic Hospitality from Raton to Deming*. Mount Pleasant, SC. Arcadia Publishing & The History Press.

Exercise

For each of the following bibliography entries, write the corresponding in-text citation using the author-date system.

Coban, Harlan. 2016. *Fool Me Once*. New York. Dutton.

_____

Stephens, Mark. 2012. *Yoga Sequencing: Designing Transformative Yoga Classes*. Berkeley, CA. North Atlantic Books.

_____

Bambrick-Santoyo, Paul. 2012. *Leverage Leadership*. Hoboken, NJ. Jossey-Bass.

_____

Bibliography

Citations in a bibliography will differ depending on the source type. There are many different source types, from print books, journals, and magazines, to websites, blogs, text messages, and emails. This section will focus on two primary source categories: print sources and digital sources.

Print Sources

Print sources are published documents such as books, encyclopedias, journals, and magazines. These sources might have online versions, but when they are cited, they are treated separately in print.

Books

When citing a book, present the information in the following order: author name, title, location, publisher, and year of publication. The location, year, and publisher are all grouped together, and a colon appears after the location. Additionally, a comma is used after the publisher.

Page numbers of cited material should be included if applicable.

The author's name should be inverted, which means that the last name comes first, followed by a comma, the first name, and any middle initials.

> Mitchell, Steve, *Legendary Locals of Estes Park*, Mt. Pleasant: Arcadia Publishing, 2016.

If a book has two or more authors, only the first listed name is inverted.

> Zimmer, Stephen, and Gene Lamm, *Colfax County*, Mt. Pleasant: Arcadia Publishing 2015.

Journal Articles

Similar to a book citation, start with the author's name. Include the article title, journal name, volume, issue number, and date of publication. Finally, include the page numbers.

> Baranello, Micaela, "Arabella, Operetta, and the Triumph of Gemütlichkeit," *The Opera Quarterly* 31, no. 4 (2015), 199 – 222.

Magazine Articles

Magazine entries are very similar to journal articles. The main difference is instead of an issue number and volume, magazines rely on dates. Where the issue number and volume are in the journal entry, instead put the month or season and date.

Del Bene, Terry A., "Deadly Flood of 1844," *True West Magazine*, April 2016, 60 – 61.

Newspaper Articles

A newspaper article entry will be almost identical to a magazine entry, except that including the date and edition is almost always necessary. Newspapers often publish daily and have various editions depending on location.

Mellskog, Pam, "Follow the Sun: How Natural Light Can Help Night Owls Reset Their Internal Clocks," *Boulder Daily Camera*, March 12, 2016.

Dictionaries and Encyclopedias

For well-known reference books and dictionaries, you need to include the name of the reference book, the edition, and the information that was referenced. The abbreviation s.v. is used prior to the reference word. It is an acronym for *sub voce* or *sub verdo*, which is Latin for "under the word" or "under the voice." This lets your audience know that they can find this reference by looking up the word following "s.v." in the dictionary cited.

The Merriam-Webster Dictionary, 10th ed., s.v. "litany."

Exercise

Read the citations below. Circle the print source that is being cited in each example.

Nicklin, Allision, "Words from the Spin Doctor: Understanding Dizziness and Vertigo," The Broadmoor, November 2015, 32 – 33.

    Book   Magazine   Dictionary

D'Aprix Sweeney, Cynthia, The Nest, New York, 2016.

    Book   Newspaper   Dictionary

Lihani, Brian, "Norad & Cheyene Mountain AFS: A New Pictorial History Book," The Cheyenne Edition, December 2015, 3.

    Book   Newspaper   Dictionary

Digital Sources

Digital sources are any sources that are available through a technological device. This can include websites, blogs, emails, and text messages.

Websites and Webpages

When citing a webpage, try to include as much information as possible: the title of the webpage, the author of the content (if any), the owner or sponsor of the site, the URL, and the publication date. If there is no publication date, choose either the date it was last updated or the access date.

"Earth Day 2016: We're not as doomed as you think," John Sutter, CNN, last modified April 22, 2016, http://www.cnn.com/2016/04/21/opinions/sutter-earth-day-hope/index.html.

Blogs

Because blogs are updated regularly, try to include as much information as possible when citing blogs. Include the author, the title of the entry, the name of the blog, and a URL.

Steve Kamb, "Real-Life Role Playing: What is your profession?" *Nerd Fitness* (blog), May 10, 2010, https://www.nerdfitness.com/blog/2010/05/10/real-life-role-playing-what-is-your-profession/.

Email/Text Messages

Include as much information as possible. Who wrote the email or text message? Who was it addressed to? Remember to include the date.

Katie Hommel, email message to Jessica Smith, January 16, 2016.

Maggie Halsey, text message to Elaine Taylor, April 21, 2016.

Exercise

Read the citations below and identify whether they are print or digital sources.

Mclaughlin, Robert, *Magic Mountain*, Mt. Pleasant: Arcadia Publishing 2016

    Print   Digital

Juli Bauer, "Fashion Fridays: Summer Must-Haves," *PaleOMG* (blog), April 22, 2016, http://paleomg.com/fashion-friday-summer-must-haves/

    Print   Digital

19c CMS Sample

The following example essay uses the notes and bibliography (NB) system.

The title is a few lines down. It ends with a colon leading into the subtitle.

Other pertinent information, such as name and course, belong a few lines below the title.

Understanding Billy the Kid:

An in-depth look at the famous outlaw

Jenni Tyler

Folklore 101, Professor Fredrickson

Understanding Billy the Kid: 1

Henry McCarty, more commonly known by his outlaw name, Billy the Kid, was an outlaw and a fugitive. He grew in infamy for his crimes and his ability to evade the law. He allegedly escaped from jail on multiple occasions and killed several men, including Lincoln County Sheriff, William Brady.1 However, Billy the Kid is touted as both a hero and a villain because, while his crimes were vast and horrendous, they were thought by some to be justified.

Billy the Kid, also referred to as William H. Bonney, was born on September 17, 1859 in New York City. Shortly after McCarty's mother married William Henry Harrison Antrim, the family relocated to Silver City, New Mexico.2 After the passing of his mother, McCarty found work at a boardinghouse. After a year under this arrangement, he left and it was then that Billy the Kid began his criminal ways. He was arrested for stealing clothing and guns, but escaped two days later.

After his first escape from prison, McCarty fled to Arizona Territory. In 1877, McCarty shot Francis "Windy" Cahill after a very heated argument.3 Cahill was known to speak in a demeaning manner to McCarty, and on this particular day, a fight ensued. In the midst of the brawl, McCarty and Cahill struggled for Cahill's gun when it went off in Cahill's direction. McCarty was again arrested for his crimes. He escaped imprisonment, stole a horse, and fled.

McCarty then found work with John Tunstall as a cowboy. Tunstall and the local lawyer, Alexander McSween, presented an opposition to the economic and political powerhouse held over Lincoln County by a trio of firearm-wielding businessmen. This began the Lincoln County War. McCarty joined the Lincoln County Regulators, a posse that banded together during the Lincoln County War to disband the trio of businessmen and avenge the murder of John Tunstall. The Regulators were indicted for the murder of Morris Bernstein, making them outlaws.

McCarty, or Billy the Kid, was finally caught and subsequently killed by Sheriff Pat Garrett, a man with a few stories of his own.4 Garrett found McCarty attempting to flee and shot

---

1 "Billy the Kid born," History.com Staff, History.com, access date April 25, 2016. http://www.history.com/this-day-in-history/billy-the-kid-born

2 "Summary of the Life of Billy the Kid," About Billy the Kid (website), last updated October, 13 2015. http://www.aboutbillythekid.com/index.html

3 John LeMay, Tall Tales & Half Truths of billy the Kid, (Arcadia Publishing & The History Press, 2015)

Headers and page numbers begin on the actual first page of the essay, not on the cover page. The header consists of the title and page number.

Note how the in-text reference corresponds with a number on the reference list.

Understanding Billy the Kid: 2

him. Billy the Kid is legend known by many, but few actually know the true story. He is most often villainized for his heinous crimes and his ability to elude punishment for those crimes, but few who have studied and know his history consider him to be a hero in disguise.

⁴ John LeMay, Tall Tales & Half Truths of Pat Garrett, (Arcadia Publishing & The History Press, 2016)

Understanding Billy the Kid: 1

Bibliography

"Billy the Kid born," History.com Staff, *History.com*, access date April 25, 2016. http://www.
history.com/this-day-in-history/billy-the-kid-born

John LeMay, *Tall Tales & Half Truths of Billy the Kid*, (Arcadia Publishing & The History Press,
2015)

---., *Tall Tales & Half Truths of Pat Garrett*, (Arcadia Publishing & The History Press, 2016)

"Summary of the Life of Billy the Kid," *About Billy the Kid* (website), last updated October, 13
2015. http://www.aboutbillythekid.com/index.html

The bibliography
should begin on a
new page.

The following example essay cited using the author-date (AD) system.

Understanding Billy the Kid:

An in-depth look at the famous outlaw

Jenni Tyler

Folklore 101, Professor Fredrickson

Understanding Billy the Kid: 2

Henry McCarty, more commonly known by his outlaw name, Billy the Kid, was an outlaw and a fugitive. He grew in infamy for his crimes and his ability to evade the law. He allegedly escaped from jail on multiple occasions and killed several men, including Lincoln County Sheriff, William Brady (History 2016). However, Billy the Kid is touted as both a hero and a villain because, while his crimes were vast and horrendous, they were thought by some to be justified.

Billy the Kid, also referred to as William H. Bonney, was born on September 17, 1859 in New York City (About Billy the Kid 2015). Shortly after McCarty's mother married William Henry Harrison Antrim, the family relocated to Silver City, New Mexico. After the passing of his mother, McCarty found work at a boardinghouse. After a year under this arrangement, he left and it was then that Billy the Kid began his criminal ways. He was arrested for stealing clothing and guns, but escaped two days later.

After his first escape from prison, McCarty fled to Arizona Territory. In 1877, McCarty shot Francis "Windy" Cahill after a very heated argument (LeMay 2015). Cahill was known to speak in a demeaning manner to McCarty, and on this particular day, a fight ensued. In the midst of the brawl, McCarty and Cahill struggled for Cahill's gun when it went off in Cahill's direction. McCarty was again arrested for his crimes. He escaped imprisonment, stole a horse, and fled.

McCarty then found work with John Tunstall as a cowboy. Tunstall and the local lawyer, Alexander McSween, presented an opposition to the economic and political powerhouse held over Lincoln County by a trio of firearm-wielding businessmen. This began the Lincoln County War. McCarty joined the Lincoln County Regulators, a posse that banded together during the Lincoln County War to disband the trio of businessmen and avenge the murder of John Tunstall. The Regulators were indicted for the murder of Morris Bernstein, making them outlaws.

McCarty, or Billy the Kid, was finally caught and subsequently killed by Sheriff Pat Garrett (LeMay 2016), a man with a few stories of his own. Garrett found McCarty attempting to flee and shot him. Billy the Kid is legend known by many, but few actually know the true story. He is most often villainized for his heinous crimes and his ability to elude punishment for those crimes, but few who have studied and know his history consider him to be a hero in disguise.

Note how the parenthetical author/date corresponds with a reference listed on the next page.

Understanding Billy the Kid: 1

References

"Billy the Kid born," History.com Staff, *History.com*, access date April 25, 2016. http://www.
history.com/this-day-in-history/billy-the-kid-born

John LeMay, *Tall Tales & Half Truths of Billy the Kid*, (Arcadia Publishing & The History Press,
2015)

---., *Tall Tales & Half Truths of Pat Garrett*, (Arcadia Publishing & The History Press, 2016)

"Summary of the Life of Billy the Kid," *About Billy the Kid* (website), last updated October, 13
2015. http://www.aboutbillythekid.com/index.html

Chapter 20

CSE

The Council of Science Editors is a non-profit organization that created an editorial style guide for writers of science-based material. It is primarily used for natural and physical sciences such as biology, chemistry, astronomy, and physics. These sciences deal with objects, laws of nature, and the physical world.

20a Formatting the Document

Like many formatting style guides, CSE has specific guidelines to follow. There are three main items to consider when formatting:

- Alignment
- Headings and page numbers
- Title page

Alignment
- The entire paper should be double-spaced
- Create one-inch margins all around

Headings and Page Numbers
- Create a header that contains the paper title
- The body of the paper should have page numbers
- End references or bibliographies should be on a separate page.
- Create and center section titles when using sections like "Discussion," "Introduction," or "Abstract"

Title Page

Essays written in CSE style should have a title page. This title page should include the title of the essay, your name, and any other important information (class name, professor, etc). All text should be center-aligned.

The title page does not need to have headers, footers, or page numbers.

Getting to Know Diabetes

Jared Henderson

Human Biology 101, Professor Martin

20b Citing the Document Sources

CSE has multiple systems for documenting sources. Depending on the preference of your audience or instructor and the discipline you're working in, you may need to use a different system each time. The three methods are listed below:

- Citation-name
- Citation-sequence
- Name-year

Each of these systems uses in-text references that point to a reference list at the end of the text.

Citation-Name

The citation-name system lists the sources alphabetically by authors' last names in the reference list at the end of the paper. The in-text reference is then numbered to match the name. This style is best to use when a reference list is primarily made up of author-listed online content.

> Benjamin Franklin's invention of the lightning rod was a direct result of his first experiment. In this experiment he hypothesized that lightning is a source of electricity and intended to prove it by creating a spark.[3] Franklin took his kite out during a storm, and lightning hit the kite, catching the contraption on fire. The lightning rod was then conceived to keep houses from being struck by lightning.[1] The rods were placed on the roofs of houses and fashioned so the lightning struck the ground rather than the house itself.[2]

References

1. Allison, A. The real Benjamin Franklin. 1. Malta, ID. National Center for Constitutional Studies. 1982. 504 pp.

2. Franklin, B. The autobiography of Benjamin Franklin. 1. Mineola, NY. Dover Publications. 1996. 144 pp.

3. Walter, I. Benjamin Franklin: an American life. 1. New York, NY. Simon & Schuster. 2003. 586 pp.

Citation-Sequence

The citation-sequence system lists the sources chronologically in the order they appear in the text. This system is best for a reference list made up primarily of online content that may or may not have an author listed.

> Benjamin Franklin's invention of the lightning rod was a direct result of his first experiment. In this experiment he hypothesized that lightning is a source of electricity and intended to prove it by creating a spark.[1] Franklin took his kite out during a storm, and lightning hit the kite, catching the contraption on fire. The lightning rod was then conceived to keep houses from being struck by lightning.[2] The rods were placed on the roofs of houses and fashioned so the lightning struck the ground rather than the house itself.[3]

References

Franklin, B. The autobiography of Benjamin Franklin. 1. Mineola, NY. Dover Publications. 1996. 144 pp.

Allison, A. The real Benjamin Franklin. 1. Malta, ID. National Center for Constitutional Studies. 1982. 504 pp.

Walter, I. Benjamin Franklin: an American life. 1. New York, NY. Simon & Schuster. 2003. 586 pp.

Name-Year

The name-year system lists the name and the year of the source in-text. This system is best used for reference lists that are primarily made up of printed materials.

> Benjamin Franklin's invention of the lightning rod was a direct result of his first experiment. In this experiment he hypothesized that lightning is a source of electricity and intended to prove it by creating a spark (Allison 1982). Franklin took his kite out during a storm, and lightning hit the kite, catching the contraption on fire. The lightning rod was then conceived to keep houses from being struck by lightning (Walter 2003). The rods were placed on the

roofs of houses and fashioned so the end point struck the ground, rather than the house itself (Franklin 1996).

References

Allison, A. The real Benjamin Franklin. 1. Malta, ID. National Center for Constitutional Studies. 1982. 504 pp.

Franklin, B. The autobiography of Benjamin Franklin. 1. Mineola, NY. Dover Publications. 1996. 144 pp.

Walter, I. Benjamin Franklin: an American life. 1. New York, NY. Simon & Schuster. 2003. 586 pp.

Exercise

Read the following citations and circle the citation method that each one is using.

"Eating smaller, more frequent meals helps keep blood sugar stable and reduces sugar cravings" (Gottlieb 2008).

    1. Name-Year   2. Citation-Name

"Maximal adult height seemed to be dependent on genetic factors, but more importantly upon nutritional factors."[1]

    1. Name-Year   2. Citation-Name

Bibliography

Citations will differ depending on the source type. There are many different source types, from print books, journals, and magazines to websites, blogs, text messages, and emails. This section will focus on two primary source categories: print sources and digital sources.

Formatting Basics

The author's name should always be inverted.

Not Inverted: Terry Pratchett

Inverted: Pratchett, T.

For books with multiple authors, only invert the first author's name and write the others normally. Authors' first names should be initials rather than written out.

Only the first word of a work should be capitalized. To save space, journal titles are abbreviated and there is no space between publication dates, volume numbers, and issues.

Print Sources

Below is the basic entry format for each source type, followed by an example.

Books

Author(s). Title. Edition. Place of publication: publisher; date. Extent.

> Munroe, R. What if? Serious scientific answers to absurd hypothetical questions. New York, NY: Houghton Mifflin Harcourt; 2014.320.

Encyclopedias/Reference Books/Textbooks

Author(s). Chapter title. In: Editor(s). Edition. Book title. Place of publication: publisher; year. Page numbers for that chapter.

> Tarbuck, E.J., F.K., Lutgens, D.G. Tasa. Earth science. 13th ed. Upper Saddle River, NJ: Pearson; 2011.300 – 321.

Magazines/Journals

Author(s). Article title. Abbreviated journal title. Date; volume(issue): pages.

> Katzer, A., S. Hockertz, G.H. Buchhorn, J.F. Loehr. In vitro toxicity and mutagenicity of *CoCrMo* and *Ti6Al* wear particles. J. Toxicol. 2003;190(3):145 – 154.

Digital Sources

Websites

Author. Titles [Internet]. Location. Publisher. Date published [date cited]. Available from: URL

Rosen, M. Beetle saved in amber had helicopter wings [Internet]. Washington, D.C. 2016 Apr 16 [cited 2016 Apr 27]. Available from: https://www.sciencenews.org/article/beetle-saved-amber-had-helicopter-wings?tgt=nr

20c CSE Sample

In this section you will find three sample essays, each utilizing a different citation style. Take note of the differences in each piece.

The following example essay is cited using the citation-name method.

Reversing Diabetes

Jared Henderson

Human Physiology 102, Professor Martin

Title page consists of a title, the author's name, and any other pertinent information. All text on the title page is centered.

Headers and page
numbers begin on
the first page of the
essay, after the title
page.

Diabetes is a chronic condition that affects the way a body handles sugar or glucose. When people eat, their glucose levels rise, and the hormone insulin is released from the pancreas into the bloodstream. Insulin acts as a door-opener, allowing the glucose to enter the cells so that it can be transformed into energy for the body. However, diabetics lack the key for this door-opening ability. The body's blood-glucose levels rise higher than normal and the body cannot properly utilize insulin to manage the elevated blood glucose levels. This is called insulin resistance.[2] Diabetics who have higher than normal levels of insulin resistance are prescribed insulin injections to take daily. Insulin dependency has been touted as a lifelong commitment, but recent studies are proving that to be false. Insulin dependency can be reversed by fostering a healthy lifestyle.

There are two types of diabetes. Type 1 diabetes is often called juvenile diabetes, as it is usually diagnosed in children or teenagers. Type 1 diabetes occurs when the body does not produce insulin. Type 2 diabetes, also called adult-onset diabetes, is when the body creates insulin but the cells do not properly digest the glucose in the bloodstream.[3] Type 1 diabetes is incurable, but some physicians believe that type 2 can be reversed.

The main causes of diabetes are genetics and obesity.[4] Genetic propensity to become diabetic is based on family history and ethnicity. Obesity, caused by high caloric intake and physical inactivity, often leads to insulin resistance because the body cannot produce enough insulin to support the higher levels of sugar entering the body.

This is where the theory of insulin-dependent reversal comes in. If a person with diabetes consumes foods that require less insulin to be digested, the body, in theory, will be capable of digesting a smaller amount of glucose and turning it into energy. Foods with lower glucose levels are vegetables, whole grains, legumes, and lean proteins. Removing common carbohydrates like processed wheat, sugary foods and drinks, foods containing high fructose corn syrup, and other foods lacking in nutritional value will blood glucose levels significantly, thus allowing the body's natural levels of insulin to work properly.[1]

Physical activity can also reverse insulin dependency because muscles use glucose more efficiently than fat.[1] Using muscles through exercise will help the body absorb the blood glucose. In addition, exercise helps keep one's body in the target blood glucose range, creating less of a need for more insulin production.

Diabetes, or insulin resistance, is a long-term chronic condition with which many people suffer. However, with proper nutrition and a regulated exercise regimen, insulin dependency in people with type 2 diabetes can be reversed.

References

References are
listed on a separate
page.

1. Collins, S. Can you reverse type 2 diabetes? [Internet]. Atlanta, GA. WebMD. 2016 Jan 10 [cited: 2016 Apr 27]. Available from: http://www.webmd.com/diabetes/type-2-diabetes-guide/reversing-type-2-diabetes?page=2

2. Diabetes. Bethesda, MD. National Institute of Health (NIH). 2015 Aug 12 [cited: 2016 Apr 27]. Available from: https://www.nlm.nih.gov/medlineplus/diabetes.html

3. Facts about type 2 [Internet]. Alexandria, VA. 2013 Aug 1 [cited 2016 Apr 27]. Available from: http://www.diabetes.org/diabetes-basics/type-2/facts-about-type-2.html?loc=db-slabnav

4. What causes diabetes? [Internet]. New York. Department of Health. 2015 Jan [cited: 2016 Apr 27]. Available from: https://www.health.ny.gov/diseases/conditions/diabetes/what_causes_diabetes.htm

The following example essay is cited using the citation-sequence method.

Understanding Diabetes

Jared Henderson

Human Physiology 102, Professor Martin

Understanding Diabetes   1

   Diabetes is a chronic disease that causes the body's glucose levels to rise higher than normal so that the body does not create enough—or properly use—insulin to break down the glucose.[1] Diabetes affects more than 30% of adults and has many causes, symptoms, and treatment options.

   Glucose is more commonly known as sugar. Glucose is in many foods, including fruit, bread, and pasta. When these foods are digested, they are turned into sugar and absorbed into the bloodstream to be converted into energy. The bodies of Individuals with diabetes are unable to convert the sugar in the bloodstream into energy due to insulin resistance. Insulin is a hormone, or "chemical messenger," created in the pancreas.[2] Insulin acts as a key, unlocking the glucose's natural energy and allowing that energy to flow into the bloodstream; unfortunately, people with diabetes do not hold the key. Often, insulin resistance is a matter of overconsumption. If there is too much sugar in the bloodstream, meaning an individual has consumed too much glucose, the body might not be able to produce enough insulin to break down the glucose.

   There are a multitude of treatments for diabetes available, ranging from all-natural to chemical medications. The majority of people with diabetes are prescribed insulin shots and medication. Insulin shots are made of pork pancreas or synthetically created to be identical to human insulin.[3] The insulin is injected directly into the fat under the skin. Insulin cannot be ingested, as the body's natural digestion process will break it down before it enters the bloodstream.

   Natural remedies range from simply eating more healthfully and exercising to taking all-natural supplements such as ginseng, magnesium, and chromium. Diet and exercise can help lower the amounts of glucose in the body, therefore making it easier for the body to produce enough insulin. Some believe that ginseng helps prevent blood-sugar levels from rising after eating. Magnesium is touted to assist insulin production, and chromium is believed to reduce blood-sugar levels.[4] However, the efficacy of these supplements has not been scientifically proven.

   Diabetes is a disease that many Americans currently face. Insulin resistance comes in many forms and has many causes. Treatment options are available, but there is no official cure for diabetes.

Understanding Diabetes   1

References

1. Type 2 [Internet]. American Diabetes Association. Alexandria, VA. c2016 [cited 30 Apr 2016]. Available from: http://www.diabetes.org/diabetes-basics/type-2/?loc=hottopics

2. Hess-Fischel, A. What is insulin? [Internet]. EndocrineWeb. Montclair, NJ. Last updated 6 Apr 2016 [cited 29 Apr 2016]. Available from: http://www.endocrineweb.com/conditions/type-1-diabetes/what-insulin

3. Insulin administration [Internet}. Diabetes Care. Jan 24;27(1).

4. Orenstein, B.W. 9 supplements that may help diabetes. Everyday Health. Last updated 29 Aug 2011 [cited 29 Apr 2016]. Available from: http://www.everydayhealth.com/type-2-diabetes/9-supplements-that-may-help-diabetes.aspx

The following example essay is cited using the name-year method.

Reversing Diabetes
Jared Henderson

Human Physiology 102, Professor Martin

Reversing Diabetes   1

Diabetes either directly or indirectly affects nearly everyone in America.

> Diabetes mellitus is a chronic disease that causes serious health complications
> including renal (kidney) failure, heart disease, stroke, and blindness....
> Approximately 30 percent of adults older than 60 have been diagnosed with diabetes,
> and its prevalence is the same in men and women.... The standard American diet
> (SAD) causes susceptible individuals to develop diabetes. (Fuhrman 2013)

 Diabetes is a problem in today's society, but research is now proving that type 2 diabetes can be reversed or "cured" through lifestyle changes.

 The primary reason an individual develops diabetes is the lack of nutrient-rich foods readily available in the standard American diet. As a culture, Americans have focused on a lifestyle of immediate gratification. This is evident in all aspects of American culture. Microwaves cook food faster than ovens. Text messages make conversations faster than phone calls. Even news articles are now condensed and filled with photographs to keep readers interested long enough to determine the main point of an article. If something requires too many steps, the majority of Americans will avoid it. This includes food. As a result, the American diet consists mainly of foods that can be eaten immediately or heated up in a microwave. These foods are filled with chemical preservatives and lack the nutrients of natural foods.

 The obvious solution would be to eat more nutrient-dense foods. However, multiple studies show certain types of foods are more harmful than others and should be avoided altogether. Carbohydrates, for example, are often touted as being bad for people with diabetes because carbohydrates turn into glucose and enter the bloodstream. Since the bodies of diabetic individuals are unable to break down high levels of glucose in the bloodstream (due to a lack of insulin or insulin that doesn't work properly), researchers think the best solution is to restrict carbohydrates. However, not all carbohydrates are the same. Healthy carbohydrates, such as whole grain, contain copious amounts of highly beneficial fiber. Fiber has been proven to slow down insulin resistance as well as a host of other diseases and health complications (Whitaker 1987).

 Another strategy for "curing" diabetes is to add exercise. Americans have grown sedentary. Most jobs require an individual to sit at a desk for hours at a time. However, muscles burn the majority of the insulin-mediated glucose that the body has consumed (Flippin 2014). Muscles will, therefore, lose insulin sensitivity caused by added fat and inflammation. The body needs daily aerobic exercise and a few strength training sessions per week to help the body metabolize more efficiently.

Diabetes can be reversed. The standard American diet and lifestyle are largely to blame for the prevalence of diabetes in modern society. However, through simple lifestyle changes like moving more, eating more nutrient-dense foods, and consuming less processed food, individuals can reduce insulin dependency.

Reversing Diabetes   1

References

Flippin, R. 2014. The diabetes reset. New York (NY): Workman Publishing Company 326 p.

Fuhrman, J. 2013. The end of diabetes. New York (NY): HarperCollins 314 p.

Whitaker, J. 1987. Reversing diabetes. New York (NY): Hachette Book Group 512 p.

Notes

Notes

otes

Notes